Praise for *Live F*

Kendra Smiley is a warm, witty, ᴀ
encouraging women to make choices that empower and encou.
age us to be all God has intended us to be! Her newest
book, *Live Free*, is a must-read for anyone who has felt entan-
gled by fear, insecurity, or just plain weariness. Today, why not
make your first good choice to live with purpose and passion
by getting this book!
 —LUCINDA SECREST MCDOWELL, speaker and author of
  Role of a Lifetime

Kendra writes what she lives! These stories are powerful
reminders of how God works all things together for His glory!
 —GEORGIA SHAFFER, author of *Taking Out Your Emotional
  Trash*, certified life coach, and licensed psychologist

This book is a must-read for all women! The stories are more
than inspirational—they're true pictures of how we need to
respond to life's if onlys and what ifs. It's the next best thing to
having Kendra move in with you!
 —VIRELLE KIDDER, conference speaker, author, CWG mentor

Kendra Smiley's excellent book will help you purge the emotional clutter that is keeping you from the life God has waiting for you!
 —CYNDY SALZMANN, America's Clutter Coach and author
  of *Making Your Home a Haven*

Kendra does a great job of challenging each one of us to eliminate the if onlys and what ifs of life—the circumstances we
all have that can keep us from the freedom God promises. Pick
up this book today and start to *Live Free*!
 —CAROLE LEWIS, First Place 4 Health National Director,
  author of *A Thankful Heart, Give God a Year,* and *Hope
  4 You*

Live Free is a collection of powerful, true stories of ordinary women who made extraordinary decisions. We all face difficult situations in life and in her writing and speaking Kendra encourages us to make the next right choice.

> —LESLIE VERNICK, licensed counselor, coach, speaker, and author of *Lord, I Just Want to be Happy* and *The Emotionally Destructive Relationship*

Live Free will show you how you can move beyond the obstacles and challenges we all face in life. Kendra's inspiring style comes through each story as she offers spiritual encouragement and practical insight. I wish I'd had this book years ago.

> —SANDRA ALDRICH, author of *From One Single Mother to Another*

Kendra Smiley shows women how to climb out of the if onlys and what ifs of their lives into a world where God is in control —if we simply ask Him.

> —DIANN MILLS, author of *Expect an Adventure* and *The Chase*

With wisdom, humor, and hope, Kendra's book *Live Free* inspires women to make choices in the midst of life's challenges that will impact their life and destiny in ways that bring glory to God.

> —CHERI FULLER, speaker and author of *A Busy Woman's Guide to Prayer* and many others

LIVE FREE

Eliminate the If Onlys and What Ifs of Life

KENDRA SMILEY

MOODY PUBLISHERS

CHICAGO

Edited by: Annette Laplaca
Interior design: Ragont Design
Cover design: Ragont Design, Mary Bellus
Cover image: iStockphoto

ISBN: 978-0-8024-0646-0

We hope you enjoy this book from Moody Publishers. Our goal is to provide high-quality, thought-provoking books and products that connect truth to your real needs and challenges. For more information on other books and products written and produced from a biblical perspective, go to www.moodypublishers.com or write to:

Moody Publishers
820 N. LaSalle Boulevard
Chicago, IL 60610

3 5 7 9 10 8 6 4 2

Printed in the United States of America

To my husband, John, who
continually models Christ to me

CONTENTS

FOREWORD

It was a relaxing August afternoon. Several writers and speakers had come together in Dallas for training in software that would be helpful as we do research for future projects. After working hard, we had an off-site break for networking and "girl time." I got in the van for the return trip to the hotel, and Kendra Smiley was my seatmate.

Catching up with my friend was a joy, and I felt comfortable enough to ask a personal question. Kendra knew our son was incarcerated with a life sentence and that his wife had left the state with our two precious step-granddaughters six years earlier. I told Kendra my husband and I had been sending birthday and Christmas gifts to the girls for the past six years, but we never heard whether or not they were received. Since the girls are now in their late teens, I asked Kendra's advice about how long we should continue giving to the girls. Without hesitation, she looked up and said, "Never quit giving to them—even if you never get a response. They will always be assured of your love."

One month later my husband and I were returning home from a speaking engagement and we had a layover in Atlanta. Gene's cell phone rang, and a soft voice on the other end of the line said, "Grampy, this is Chelsea. I'm nineteen years old and I'm a freshman in college. I want my family back." Tears flowed on both ends of the call that day, and two months later we had a glorious reunion. Kendra Smiley had helped me make a choice that will forever change the rest of my life for the better.

This book is filled with true stories of people who have chosen forgiveness, joy, contentment, prayer, and positive attitudes that resulted in renewed hope, increased faith, and purposeful action. You will laugh and wipe a tear or two as you read each chapter. I plan to share this book with family members and friends who will be encouraged to make godly decisions in the midst of their own personal challenges.

Kendra Smiley inspires us through her public speaking, through her radio program, and through her written words to hold on to hope and to make decisions based on biblical truth. I highly recommend her profound ministry as she helps each of us make the next right choice.

Carol Kent
Speaker and author of *When I Lay My Isaac Down*
(NavPress)
and *Between a Rock and a Grace Place* (Zondervan)

1

IF
ONLY

Watch for big problems; they disguise
big opportunities.

H. JACKSON BROWN, *LIFE'S LITTLE INSTRUCTION BOOK*

It was 7:15 on a beautiful Sunday morning. I was sitting at the island in our kitchen having a cup of tea when the phone rang.

"Good morning," I said cheerfully.

The caller was hesitant. Finally a muffled voice sobbed into the receiver.

"Kendra," the man said emotionally, "this is Steve. Pam asked me to call you."

Pam is a dear friend and sister in Christ. Our distant locations and busy lives prohibit frequent visits, but we stay in touch by phone calls, email, and texting.

My mind raced as I tried to determine what had prompted this tearful call. Something was wrong, and I literally held my breath as he continued.

"It's about Emily."

Emily was their new baby, their third daughter, and she was just four months old. She was obviously in trouble, but what was wrong? My mind began to race again, wondering what might have happened to trigger the call.

"We need you to pray," Steve sobbed. "She was just diagnosed with an inoperable brain tumor."

For a moment I was too shocked to respond. In all my imagining, I had not thought of this happening. How was it possible? How could someone so young and so innocent have a condition considered by medical experts to be so rare?

"What? Tell me more," I replied. Secretly I hoped I had not heard him correctly, that I had misunderstood his words and his tone.

"Emily has been having problems for about three weeks. We have had her examined by several physicians, and up until this point they had no clue as to the problem. Just this morning it was determined that her illness is the result of a brain tumor," Steve explained with patience and with pain.

"Why can't they take it out? Why is it inoperable?" I asked, still unable to grasp what I was hearing.

"It is a vascular tumor, one surrounded by blood vessels. If they remove it, they are sure Emily will bleed to death," he said, beginning to cry once again.

Steve, the father of this critically ill baby, had been sent to the phone to call a list of prayer warriors. My name was just one on the list.

*   *   *

When one door of happiness closes, another opens;

but often we look so long at the closed door

that we do not see the one that has been opened for us.

Helen Keller

*   *   *

It was February and time once again for the Sunday school convention. For several years, Shirley and I had helped at the convention and shared a hotel room.

It was always a treat to be with Shirley. Her wit and enthusiasm made our job at the book table fun and our time off even more enjoyable. She was a good friend and a mentor to me in my faith.

During a particularly long break, Shirley and I went to our hotel room to rest and talk. The convention was going well. Book sales were ringing in, and we had been having fun.

We took off our shoes, got as comfortable as we could on the hotel furniture, and started to visit. We talked about Shirley's two teenage kids—about their plans and their futures—and about my younger kids. We talked about how spectacular our husbands were and how fortunate we were. We laughed and we cried. There was nothing unusual in our doing these things, except that possibly we laughed a little less than usual and cried a little more.

This was, you see, a monumental day in Shirley's life. It was not monumental in the sense of accomplishment or rewards. It was monumental in another way. When we got to our room that afternoon, before we shared our thoughts and our dreams with one another, Shirley combed her hair and it began to fall out in handfuls from her recent chemotherapy.

Only weeks before, Shirley had gone to the hospital to have a benign lump removed and had instead undergone a radical mastectomy. Her chemotherapy had begun, and after one session she was losing her hair. Shirley was prepared for her hair loss in a practical way. She had a wig for public events and a turban for private moments. But she was not prepared in an emotional sense.

We cried together as we mourned the physical losses Shirley had already endured and thought of the many events yet to come that were too precious for Shirley to miss.

*   *   *

When you can't change
the direction of the wind,
adjust your sails.
Max DuPree

*   *   *

"I got married with a very idealistic view of marriage," Betty reflected. "You know, the little house with the white picket fence and everybody living happily ever after. By the time I realized that this wasn't true in my case and admitted to myself that my husband was not only an unbeliever (contrary to what he had told me prior to the wedding) but was also physically abusive, I already had children. I wanted them to experience as ideal an atmosphere as possible. And making sure they did became my mission. I could not worry about the things I could not change.

*   *   *

God is in charge.
Every disappointment is His appointment.
Kay Arthur

*   *   *

"I remember lying in my bed one night and realizing Pete was not going to be the father he was supposed to be. I knew that, and I knew I had to go forward and do what I could to be a good mother to my children. I wanted them to have a Christian home and a church. In the spiritual sense, I was responsible for these young lives. I needed to teach them the ways of the Lord and bring them the gospel. That was my responsibility. I also had to understand that I was not responsible for my husband's salvation or his parenting. So I said to God, 'I'll be

14

their mother, but you're going to have to be their Father. They don't have a father who will pray with them or read the Bible to them or teach them about You. You are going to have to father them. I'm not going to worry. I know You will meet their needs.'"

What do these real-life stories have in common? Steve and Pam faced a life-and-death situation with their baby daughter; Shirley was battling cancer; Betty found herself in an unhealthy, unhappy marriage. The common thread is that each situation had the potential to be a big "if only."

> If only our daughter were not so ill . . .
> If only my health were restored . . .
> If only I had a loving husband . . .
> If only.

"If onlys" have existed since ancient times. In Old Testament days, Joseph had a lengthy list of possible "if onlys." Remember his story? Joseph's father, Jacob, preferred him over his brothers. He was Dad's favorite, and to illustrate this fact, Jacob gave Joseph a stunning coat of many colors. His older brothers were jealous, and they threw him into a pit and then sold him into slavery.

There were more "if onlys." Joseph was taken to a foreign land by the slave traders. There he diligently served Potiphar, the second in command of the nation. Potiphar's wife propositioned Joseph, and when he resisted, she lied and claimed he had assaulted her. Joseph was thrown into prison for an unspecified sentence, with no appeals.

If only Joseph had been given a lighter jail sentence. If only Potiphar's wife had been truthful. If only she had been attracted to the gardener instead. If only the slave traders had taken a different route that day. If only Joseph's brothers had thrown him into a creek or a stream. If only Jacob had made several coats of many colors. Joseph's list of "if onlys" could have been quite long.

Now let's take a look at Esther. Here is another Old Testament star who had plenty of opportunities for "if onlys." A quick review reminds us that Esther was a beautiful young woman raised in Persia by her cousin Mordecai. At a young age she was chosen by the king to be his wife. This position was not all glitz and glamour, however. The king had some pretty frightening traditions. For example, if someone entered his chamber without being called, the king had the option of recognizing him with the extension of his scepter, or ignoring him, which meant "off with his (or her) head."

Haman, the king's right-hand man, had an intense dislike for the Jews. After Esther's cousin Mordecai refused to bow to Haman (or to anyone else but God), Haman's self-proclaimed mission became the annihilation of the Jews. Through trickery, Haman was able to convince the king to sanction his plan for Jewish destruction. Neither Haman nor the king knew that the queen was a Jew.

The plot thickened until ultimately Mordecai insisted Queen Esther enter the king's chambers with a plan to stop Haman. (Remember that if she were not officially recognized by the king, she would not have to worry about repeating the mistake.)

If only Mordecai had another plan. If only Esther could find someone else to stop Haman's evil. If only the king were a little more tolerant of unannounced visitors. If only she weren't the queen of Persia. The list could go on and on.

Do you have an "if only" in your life? If only your parents had appreciated your talent as much as they did your brother's. If only your father hadn't left your mother. If only your mother hadn't been an alcoholic. If only your income were greater. If only you didn't live in _____ (fill in the blank). If only your husband were more affectionate. If only you weren't alone.

We could go on and on. There is an unending list of possible "if onlys." Some of them you have created yourself (if only you hadn't married the one you did). Some are beyond our control (if only you hadn't been the firstborn child). Some are seemingly insignificant (if only your garage were bigger), and some are monumental (if only you could conceive a child).

An "if only" has the potential to assume a tremendous amount of power. If unleashed, an "if only" can overtake your attitudes and control your choices. The good news is that you can determine whether to give the "if only" control.

Joseph had a lot of "if onlys" from which he could choose. All of those things could have justified Joseph having a bad attitude, being jealous, or lacking confidence. But Joseph chose not to allow the "if onlys" to dictate his attitude. He made the choice not to let the "if onlys" control his future.

Esther requested that the Jewish community join her in prayer and fasting for three days before she approached the king. She did not dwell on her possible "if onlys." She did not let them control her actions, attitudes, or confidence. She was not gripped by fear. Instead she chose not to worry and to believe, with her cousin Mordecai, that perhaps she was made queen "for such a time as this" (Esther 4:14).

Do you want your circumstances, your "if onlys," to control your attitude and rule your life? Or do you want to make choices that can lead to a positive, Christ-like attitude?

I know *my* answer to these questions. If I chose to, I could make a pretty impressive list of "if onlys" of my own. Unpleasant things have happened in my life from time to time, creating "if onlys" that could justify a bad attitude. Rather than let those things control my life and create resentment, however, I prefer to make choices that will result in a positive attitude. Choices for a positive attitude are much more productive and much more pleasant than choices that allow the "if onlys" to take control.

*   *   *

**Experience is not what happens to a man,
it's what a man does with what happens to him.**

James Huxley

*   *   *

After speaking to a group of gourmet cooks several years ago (not about cooking but about working with people), I acquired a wonderful recipe for garlic bread sticks. I must pause at this point and tell you how I define a "wonderful recipe." First, it must taste good. Second, it must involve very little work but give the illusion that I am a good cook. This particular recipe met both criteria, and the finished product looked great too! It was a wonderful recipe.

We were having a potluck for our Sunday school class the next week. Traditionally, I determine what I will bring to a potluck by frantically running to the pantry an hour before the event and trying to decide what I can make with what I have on hand. I am unique in that way within my church. Most of my girlfriends are spectacular cooks. (My definition of "spectacular cooks": The dish they bring to the potluck not only tastes good but also looks like it could be photographed for *Better Homes and Gardens*.)

I decided that this time I would actually plan ahead. I purchased the ingredients for the garlic bread sticks, followed the recipe, and prepared them (in bulk) as my offering for the evening. When we arrived at the potluck, I unobtrusively placed my bread sticks in the long line of delicious food. Almost everyone sampled them.

"Oooo! These bread sticks are delicious! Barb, did you bring these?"

"No? Loretta, did you make these great bread sticks?"

"You didn't? Sue, are these from your kitchen?"

This questioning continued until finally I couldn't stand it.

18

"Someone ask me if I made the bread sticks," I demanded. At first no one responded. I guess they were in shock at the thought.

Finally, in disbelief, someone asked, "Kendra, did you make the bread sticks?" By then everyone had guessed the answer to the question. I had made the bread sticks. I had a good recipe with quality ingredients, and I chose to follow it.

Although I am no culinary wizard, I have learned through more than thirty years of marriage and raising a family that with a good recipe (which I actually follow) even *I* can be a good cook.

So read on, and I will share with you several choices you can make to maintain the attitude that the Word commands. These choices are like the ingredients in a wonderful recipe, but—just like my famous bread stick recipe—you must use the specified ingredients and you must follow the recipe.

We'll see how Steve and Pam, Shirley, Betty, and many others have made choices that have resulted in a Christ-like attitude in spite of their circumstances and in spite of their potential "if onlys."

You, too, can triumph over your "if onlys" and make choices that will lead to a positive attitude.

*   *   *

**Forgetting what is behind and straining
toward what is ahead, I press on.**

Philippians 3:13–14

*   *   *

STUDY QUESTIONS

If Only

1. Can you think of a time when you started a sentence with the words If Only or What If? How did you finish that sentence?

2. How do "If Onlys" and "What Ifs" control your actions and decisions?

3. Read and reflect on Philippians 3:12–16. What are the key words Paul uses to press on?

2

CHOOSE
TO FORGIVE

Forgiveness ought to be like a concealed
note—torn in two and burned up,
so that it never can be shown against one.

HENRY WARD BEECHER

I grew up in a small town in the middle of America, the youngest of three children. We had an upright home, and the standards for honesty, justice, morality, and language were high. It was not, however, a Christian home, and church did not play a significant part in our family life.

My father was a dentist and a pillar of the community (whatever that is). My mom was a homemaker. Like most married couples, they were as different from each other as night and day. Mom had been raised in an affluent, bilingual, German-American home. She was very regimented in her life. If she bought my sister a blouse for Christmas that cost $30 and got me a robe for $29.95, she would want to tape the nickel difference to the tag.

Dad grew up in an impoverished home. When he decided to go to dental school in the early 1930s, his parents sent him off to school with a handshake. That's all they could afford to give him. In order to pay for dental school, he red-capped at Union Station in Chicago, carrying bags for the passengers on the trains. Occasionally he could not afford to continue immediately into the next semester but was forced to work for a few months instead. After he finally graduated, he helped his younger brother complete dental school.

Dad's dental office was old-fashioned. There is a great possibility that many of you have never been inside an office like my dad's. The front door was a screen door on a spring. Attached at the top of the door was a little cowbell that clanged as the door banged shut. It was there to greet you and to let Dad and his assistant know that a patient had arrived. Down the hall was Dad's operating room. The chair was made of steel and had very little padding. No recliners for this office. (The recliners in dentists' offices today suggest that you will feel relaxed and will have a great time. At least Dad's chair didn't lie.) The light above the chair was big and glaring, blinding you into submission.

Dad was a left-handed dentist. He contended that there had been no provision for teaching left-handed dentists when he was learning. This meant he maneuvered himself into an awkward position as he stood at the right-handed chair. He reached across his patients and simulated half a bear hug. Furthermore, he was shaped a little like I have been on three occasions in my life—right before the birth of each of my three sons. This meant that as he examined your teeth, he gave you half a hug and you rested your ear on his tummy. (I found it very comforting and did not realize this was the least bit unusual—until I had a skinny, right-handed dentist.)

Dad's office was old-fashioned, his technique was old-fashioned, and so was his generosity. Dad was hardworking and generous, maybe generous to a fault.

Dad practiced dentistry long before the establishment of Medicare and federal assistance. The basic philosophy at his dental practice went something like this: "If you have a toothache, you need a dentist. I am a dentist. I'll do everything I can do to help you, and later we'll figure out how you can pay for it." Pretty generous, huh?

When my sister and brother were young, Dad had a patient who paid for her dental work in live chickens. These were delivered to our home (in town!), where my dad swiftly chopped off their heads. Rumor has it that there was more than one nightmare resulting from that payment.

I don't remember the chickens, but I do recall the woman who paid for her dentures in raspberries. I realize that raspberries are expensive, but according to my calculations, she should still be bringing raspberries to my father's heirs each year.

It didn't matter to Dad. He didn't keep score. He was generous and fun and kind. And he was also an alcoholic. I always like to make sure that I present some of the positive things about Dad before I let people know that last piece of information.

Maybe you are the way I used to be. I had some real misconceptions about alcoholism. First of all, I thought alcoholics didn't live in small towns; they lived in metropolitan areas—big cities. Their addresses were something like 234 S. Skid Row. Alcoholics weren't professionals. Weren't alcoholics usually unemployed? Alcoholics definitely were not "pillars of the community." They didn't have nice families. Their kids didn't go to college. And they all drank some mysterious liquor from a container hidden in a paper bag. Is this what you think too? Wrong!

Alcoholics live in small towns and in big cities—on Country Club Boulevard and on skid row. They are doctors and lawyers and teachers and plumbers and construction workers. They are employed, unemployed, and employers. They are pillars of the community and drifters. Alcoholics have nice families and no families. Their kids are like any other kids. And alcoholics drink bargain basement liquor and the fancy stuff too.

Alcoholics are brothers and fathers and sons and mothers and sisters and daughters and grandfathers and grandmothers and nephews and nieces and husbands and wives. In fact, as you read this sentence today, there is a 25 percent chance that alcoholism has personally touched your life in some way.

If alcoholism has touched your life, you know exactly what I mean when I tell you my stomach would knot at the slightest whiff of alcohol. It didn't even have to be hard liquor. My husband has declared, more than once, that I could detect a teaspoon of "near beer" on the breath of a passerby.

Maybe I can. You get conditioned to things like that when you live with an alcoholic. You can also become a master of denial. Denial is a skill I developed to a high level. I was so good at it, in fact, that I would not even admit the existence of the alcohol problem in our home. "Experts who treat alcoholism say that those people who are closest to an alcoholic are the least likely to acknowledge the existence of the alcoholism."[1]

I didn't acknowledge that there was alcoholism in my family until the day my husband brought it up. We had been married about three months and were living far from our childhood homes, thanks to the United States Air Force. One evening, we entertained another couple we had met at the base chapel. The couple was very nice, and it was fun to get to know them a little better. During the course of the evening, the man told us his mother was coming for a visit. He went on to tell us that she was an alcoholic. After they left, John and I talked.

"Isn't it sad that Brian's mom is an alcoholic?" I asked sympathetically.

John looked at me with disbelief. "Your dad is an alcoholic," he said.

I was shocked and hurt. "He is not! And don't you ever say that again!"

That ended the conversation, but it started me thinking. For the first time in my life, I contemplated the possibility that my father was an alcoholic. Little by little I started to read articles and books about alcoholism. The more I learned, the more I realized the truth in John's statement: Dad *was* an alcoholic.

The reality of that statement was powerful. Simultaneous to this amazing admission of the truth about my dad's alcoholism came an awakening of faith in Jesus Christ in my life. The combination was practically volatile.

Now that I was a Christian and knew the reality of Christ's love, I was eager to share the truth with Dad. After all, I reasoned, he needed Jesus more than anyone I had ever known. (Please forgive my shaky theology. In reality, all people have a desperate need for Jesus, regardless of their drinking habits. Alcoholism is a sad disease that negatively affects many others besides the diseased, but Dad was not going to hell any faster than the sober man who did not know Christ as his Savior.)

Before long I had the perfect opportunity to share my newfound faith. John's schedule in the military was rigorous, and he was gone from home a great deal. After much prayer, he and I made the decision that I would return home for the last semester of his training and that I would enroll for another semester toward my college degree.

Mom and Dad agreed to filling their empty nest once again, and so I went home. My mission was twofold: to finish one more semester at the university and to share the gospel with my father.

I was soon to learn that the first part of my mission was the easier part. I commuted to school each day and spent my free time between classes cramming in the library. Then each evening I would return to my parents' home and to the second part of my mission.

My prayer was a simple one: "Lord, change Dad." Fortunately, at some point I paused long enough in my requesting to listen to God. No, there was no audible voice; it was more like a thought—a thought bigger than any I could have had on my own. And God's idea was different from mine.

"Lord, change Dad," I prayed. The response seemed to be, *Let's not worry about your dad. Let me change you.* "How ridiculous! I am not the one who is drinking. I have asked you to be my Savior. I'm not the one with the problem; it's obviously Dad," I countered.

Let me change you. God's response was always the same.

The thought was a novel one. I was young in my faith, and yet I was growing. I didn't know much, but I did realize I was not as smart as God. So with a wavering confidence, I agreed to plan B. No longer did I pray, "Lord, change Dad." Instead I prayed for the willingness to let God change me.

It was difficult for me to break old patterns of behavior. I had chosen through the years to be a delightful daughter when my dad was sober and to be a sarcastic smart aleck when he had been drinking. I was growing in my faith, and the more I read the Bible, the more I realized there was no room for me to be a smart aleck. The truth was that I might be the only Bible Dad would ever read.

So, with God's help, I started to unlearn behavior I had perfected over the years. Each evening I would set aside some time to visit with Dad about my day. It was easy to do this on the days he was sober. My dad was really a fun guy. The days when he had been drinking were a challenge. I hated it when he repeated stories again and again. I hated it when he slurred his words. I hated it when he stumbled and tottered.

In order to help me curb my tongue, I developed a little trick. When my dad had been drinking and I had the urge to answer him with a rude retort, I clenched my fists and dug my fingernails into the palms of my hands. The self-inflicted pain had the desired effect. It reminded me to be kind and polite even when I didn't want to.

My plan worked, and I was able to be calm and courteous in my visits with Dad each evening. God was truly changing my responses. He was also changing my attitude. One night when I returned to my bedroom after my daily visit with my father, I noticed that the palms of my hands were not dented from routine fingernail reminders. It was an interesting discovery, and I remember thinking how nice it was that Dad had changed. Then I glanced across the hall to his room and realized there had been little change in his behavior. He had obviously been drinking that evening.

What had changed? Why didn't I have to dig my fingernails into my palms to control my tongue? The answer was as simple as the prayer I had uttered: God was changing me.

On that evening, the realization that my palms were unmarked was a rite of passage for me. My attitude had officially shifted. Instead of striving to alter Dad's behavior, I realized my job was to love him as Christ did. It wasn't always easy, but for the first time in my life I knew it was possible.

The semester passed (and so did I), and it was time to close that chapter of my life. It had been a time of tremendous healing for me. My father and I had experienced some degree of reconciliation in our relationship, and God was at work in both of our lives.

The significance of that time together increased greatly when, less than a year and a half later, my father died of stomach cancer. God had allowed me to love my father first as an act of my will and then truly as a supernatural gift from Him. That was the beginning of choosing to forgive.

You see, when you live with someone who is afflicted with the disease of alcoholism, you can accumulate many things that require forgiveness. It can take years of divine intervention before you even feel like forgiveness is making a difference. Do not grow weary. God is explicit about our choice to forgive.

"Our Father, who art in heaven, hallowed be thy name. Thy

kingdom come, thy will be done, on earth as it is in heaven. Give us this day our daily bread. And forgive us our trespasses as we forgive those who trespass against us."

In this prayer, we ask God to forgive us in the same manner we forgive others. We may be tempted to think, "They don't deserve my forgiveness." Yet, I don't see a provision made for that attitude.

One of the saddest phrases I have ever heard is "I can never forgive him." It would be more truthful to say, "I choose not to forgive him." Both responses are incredibly sad.

Jesus instructs us on the more perfect choice: "'Lord, how many times shall I forgive my brother when he sins against me? Up to seven times?' Jesus answered, 'I tell you, not seven times, but seventy-seven times'" (Matthew 18:21–22). Again, there is no exemption. God's instructions are not always easy, but they are always best. The first step in forgiveness is realizing that it is God's command and His desire for us. The next step is realizing that it is our choice.

My choice of forgiveness began as an act of my will, a choice. There is no doubt in my mind that God's Holy Spirit prompted that choice. I had the ability to listen to God's Spirit and to the Word of God or to reject it. I had the choice.

I chose to be kinder in word and deed to my father. At first I needed a crutch, the pain my fingernails inflicted on the palms of my hands each time I wanted to reply in a manner less than Christ-like. But eventually I was able to respond to Dad in a kindly manner without the painful reminder.

The gospel I presented to my father was one with few words. I looked for opportunities to share my faith, but moreover, I took the opportunities provided to share my love for Christ and for my father. When he died, my heart was at peace, knowing God had worked change in me.

*   *   *

Unforgiveness does a great deal more damage
to the vessel in which it is stored
than the object on which it is poured.

S. I. McMillen

*   *   *

In my mind, my father's death was the end of the story. I had no intention of sharing with others the story of my childhood or my reconciliation with my dad. Then about four years after my father died, I enrolled in a class for speakers—a class structured to help laypeople articulate their faith, from the pulpit and in their daily lives. I felt a prompting to write a message sharing the story of the intervention of my heavenly Father in my relationship with my earthly father. The most amazing thing occurred as I prepared that message.

As I prayed and searched the Scriptures in preparation for my assignment, the Word of God leapt off the page.

> If anyone has caused grief [Dad], he has not so much grieved me as he has grieved all of you, to some extent—not to put it too severely. The punishment inflicted on him by the majority is sufficient for him. Now instead, you ought to forgive and comfort him, so that he will not be overwhelmed by excessive sorrow. I urge you, therefore, to reaffirm your love for him. The reason I wrote you was to see if you would stand the test and be obedient in everything. If you forgive anyone, I also forgive him. And what I have forgiven—if there was anything to forgive—I have forgiven in the sight of Christ for your sake, in order that Satan might not outwit us. For we are not unaware of his schemes. 2 Corinthians 2:5–11

What an amazing thing! God's Word contained the exact instructions God had put into my heart. What a confirming moment. What a victory! Satan did not outwit us in this instance.

Approximately three years later, the air force relocated John and me about two thousand miles from home. That was far enough away that I felt comfortable sharing with a small group the story of my childhood and the victorious choice God had directed in my life. The sharing was brief, and the words were not dramatic.

The next morning there was a knock on my door, and it was one of the women who had been at the Bible study the night before.

"Are you busy?" she asked. "May I come in for a few minutes?"

"Of course," I replied.

She joined me for a cup of tea and began to explain the reason for her early-morning visit. "It really hit me when you shared about your father last night. In fact, it made such an impact that my husband and I talked about it until well past midnight. You see, my dad is an alcoholic, and last night was the first time I have ever faced that truth and realized how much bitterness I have accumulated in the last twenty-five years."

Her words surprised me. It was impossible not to notice the joy in her eyes and in her heart. God had already begun the healing process of forgiveness. It was evident in her words of praise to God.

Forgiveness cannot occur when there is denial of the truth. No matter how ugly the past or how difficult the situation, God desires for us to be a forgiving people. It is our choice, and initially it is a matter of our will.

When we choose to do what is right in God's eyes, when we choose to forgive others for real or imagined wrongs, God begins a supernatural work in us. He will carry our forgiveness beyond our will to our hearts.

Several years ago, I was speaking to a group of pastors' wives at a retreat. I considered it quite a privilege to provide spiritual nourishment and refreshment for women who stood on the front lines with their husbands. I had come to the conference to minister to them through God's grace. I had no idea how God would minister to me.

My first message was "My Story: Meeting Him Personally." This is, in part, the story you have just read, about how the Lord saved me and changed my attitude from bitterness to forgiveness. My notes consisted of about five statements on a small sheet of paper. (You don't need extensive notes when you're telling about what God has done in your own life.) The outline was my road map for the message so that I could successfully navigate from the beginning to the end. As I closed the message, we all bowed our heads to pray. I spoke from my heart about my thankfulness for God's love and for His Word and for the divine appointments we have with Him in our lives. Before I knew it, I heard myself say, "And I thank You, Lord, that my father was my father."

The women who were joining me in prayer had no idea of the personal magnitude of what I had just prayed. Never before had I been able (or even chosen) to say those words. God had honored my act of obedience in forgiving and had gone far "above all that we ask or think" (Ephesians 3:20 KJV). I knew as I spoke those words that God had graciously blessed me with a more complete forgiveness for my father.

I had a choice. I could have lived with my "if onlys" in charge of my life. If only my father had not been an alcoholic. If only he had been healed of this disease before his death. If only I could be sure he had embraced the gospel and received Jesus Christ as his Savior. If only those things had happened, I might have been able to share what God had done in my life. I might have been able to help others see the benefit of forgiveness. If only . . .

Our attitude is our choice. Choose to forgive. It is the next right choice!

* * *

When God prepares to do something wonderful,

He begins with a difficulty.

When He plans to do something very wonderful,

He begins with an impossibility.

Reverend Charles Inwood

* * *

CHOOSE TO

God calls us to be forgivers. We do not forgive because those who have offended us deserve our forgiveness. We don't forgive because the offender has asked for forgiveness. We forgive because God has given us the power to make that positive choice.

We forgive because it is God's command to us: "Bear with each other and forgive whatever grievances you may have against one another. Forgive as the Lord forgave you" (Colossians 3:13). He has given us the power to choose to forgive, and that choice empowers us for godly living.

STUDY QUESTIONS
Choose to Forgive

1. Has the Lord been speaking to your heart on the issues of forgiveness?

2. Read Colossians 3:12–17. How and why are we commanded to forgive? What are you facing that makes forgiveness difficult for you?

3. Name a time when you experienced forgiveness from someone. How did it make you feel?

4. Do you ever have difficulty accepting/believing in God's forgiveness?

3

CHOOSE
TO PRAY

Pray continually.

1 THESSALONIANS 5:17

E mily was so sick—so terribly, terribly sick. Her little four-month-old body lay on the sterile white sheets, pale and listless. Her cries were weak and pitiful. There was no indication that anyone should even bother to hope. The physicians had given their edict.

"Emily has an inoperable brain tumor that we suspect is cancerous," they proclaimed. "It's surrounded by blood vessels, making it life-threatening to remove. Any attempt would mean that Emily would surely bleed to death. There is really no hope."

"I don't believe there is 'no hope,'" Emily's mother replied. "There is always hope. I've been praying, and so are many others."

It might have been more accurate to say "many, many others."

Pam and Steve had taken little Emily to their local hospital earlier that morning. Doctors had tested her for a suspected gastrointestinal problem. When the tests showed nothing specific, Emily had been sent home.

After only hours at home, however, Pam knew that Emily needed to go back to the hospital emergency room. Their pediatrician met them there and admitted her for observation. In the night Emily had a seizure, and her doctor immediately ordered a CAT scan to be done in the morning. When the scan indicated a mass on the brain, Emily and her family went by ambulance to a larger city and a better-equipped hospital.

It was then that the call went out for others to pray. Pam went through the address book in her purse and tried to think of everyone and anyone who would pray. She knew that prayer could make a difference, so she chose to enlist as many prayer partners as she could.

*   *   *

Devote yourselves to prayer,

keeping alert in it with an attitude of thanksgiving.

Colossians 4:2 NASB

*   *   *

"Of course there's hope," Pam countered. "Emily is still alive. If you won't operate, there must be someone who will."

"Give me until tomorrow," the pediatric neurologist said. "I am having difficulty separating myself from this case emotionally. Perhaps there is some option I can't see at the present time."

"We'll give you the evening to think, and we will pray for Emily and for you," Pam replied.

And pray they did! Emily's family and the hundreds of others who knew about her grave situation prayed with fervor.

"That was such a difficult time," Pam admitted. "We were waiting for the doctor to make a suggestion as to our next step.

It comforted me to envision all the prayer warriors who were hard at work. I imagined them circling the hospital and holding hands. The group was so large that it went for miles and miles. People we had called had called others," she explained. "Prayer concerns have that ripple effect. Those who are praying multiply as the concern is shared with others. Many people who did not even know us prayed for Emily. Hundreds or maybe even thousands of people prayed for her to be healed."

Remembering this army of prayer warriors and reading the Word of God calmed Pam. In the Psalms she read, "The Lord is the strength of his people, a fortress of salvation for his anointed one" (Psalm 28:8).

Then Pam had another idea.

"Steve," she declared, "we need to have the elders come from our church and anoint Emily with oil and pray for healing."

Steve agreed and sent out the request.

*   *   *

Prayer is an invisible tool

which is wielded in a visible world.

Leo Tolstoy

*   *   *

Meanwhile, as Pam and Steve waited for their church friends to assemble, they were told that if a surgical procedure were attempted, Emily might need blood. The doctors were eager to have her receive healthy blood yet were concerned about the possible contamination of the existing blood supply. Everyone in the family was tested. Pam and her mother were a perfect match.

"As we prepared to give blood, we had to complete a great deal of paperwork," Pam explained. "At one point, the technician asked for our driver's licenses. Mom had hers, but I had hurriedly climbed into the ambulance and never imagined I might need it."

"We can't take your blood without the identification of your driver's license," the lab technician explained.

"But I don't have it, and my baby is critically ill. She may need my blood," said Pam.

"I doubt if I can take it," the technician replied in an uncaring tone, "but let me make a phone call."

As she left the room to make the call, Pam prayed intently. "Lord, let them take my blood for Emily."

The technician returned and said, "I'm sorry, but there is just no way I can bend the rules. We must have your license."

Just then, an assistant appeared at the door, summoning the lab technician. "I'll be right back," she said as she left the room again.

The exit gave Pam one more opportunity to cry out to God in prayer. "Emily might need my blood, Lord. Please make it possible for me to give it."

Moments later the technician returned looking puzzled and a little chagrined. "That phone call gave me permission to go ahead and take your blood. Believe me, that has never happened before. Roll up your sleeve, please."

Pam smiled with delight. She secretly wondered if perhaps the phone call had come straight from heaven.

*   *   *

I prayed for this child,

and the Lord has granted me what I asked of him.

1 Samuel 1:27

*   *   *

By the time Pam and her mom returned to Emily's room, many of their church family had assembled. Although it was a two-hour drive, all of the elders who had been contacted had been able to gather. They circled the hospital crib of little Emily, anointed her with oil, and prayed for her healing.

In the morning the pediatric neurologist met with Pam and Steve just as he had promised. He had, in fact, come up with an option. In St. Louis there was a surgeon more daring and aggressive than the average doctor. He was also highly skilled.

"It is possible," their doctor explained, "that he will attempt the removal of Emily's tumor, if you are interested."

"We are definitely interested," Pam said. "So what do we do next?"

That question put into motion a plan to try to save Emily's life. Within a few hours, a Life Line plane was ready to take the family to St. Louis. They boarded the plane with Emily, a nurse, and the precious blood that had been miraculously gathered. Perhaps they would need this blood, if surgery were done.

En route and even before the flight, Pam and Steve prayed for guidance in making the right decisions. Before they flew to St. Louis, the first neurologist had role-played with them the possible dialogue with the surgeon. He let them know the tough presentation they might encounter and the tough call they, as parents, would have to make. Now they could do nothing more than to ask God for guidance.

In St. Louis, they were greeted by a team of specialists who examined Emily and the test records that arrived with her. Finally the consultation began.

"This is definitely a vascular tumor, but I am willing to operate," the surgeon declared. "Her chances of surviving the operation are not good. If she does survive, she runs a high risk of paralysis, blindness, and the very real possibility that the tumor will grow back. We must also consider the fact that the tumor is probably cancerous and that she will have to have chemotherapy and radiation."

The presentation was as harsh as their previous doctor had warned. There was no optimism or glimmer of hope, at least not from the team of physicians.

"So," they asked, "what is your decision?"

"We want you to operate," was the reply.

Undoubtedly the speed of the answer astounded the doctors. It did not surprise Pam and Steve though. They had been praying about what they should do and they felt the peace that passes understanding as they gave their answer.

"What were our other options?" I heard Pam ask, years later. "Really? We wanted to give Emily a chance for life. Our other option was to watch her die. It didn't seem like much of a choice."

That evening after visiting hours were over, a pastor Pam and Steve didn't know well came by the hospital.

"I'm sorry I couldn't get here any sooner," apologized Pastor Bob upon his arrival. "We have been praying though. In fact we have felt led to pray specifically that you would have wisdom and discernment. Does that make sense to you?"

It definitely made sense! While the pastor and his prayer team were praying for wisdom and discernment, Emily's parents were making their decision whether or not to allow doctors to operate on the "inoperable" brain tumor.

"God is so amazing," Pam declared. "He had people praying precisely for our needs. They didn't know us or even know why wisdom and discernment were important."

*   *   *

Evening, morning and noon I cry out in distress,

and he hears my voice.

Psalm 55:17

*   *   *

Later that night, however, Pam felt as if she were wrestling with the devil. Negative thoughts bombarded her mind, thoughts that caused her to question the decision they had made.

"How can you do this to your baby? Why don't you take

her home and have as much time as you can have with her? Why do you want to kill her like this?"

It was a rough night, but God's assurance prevailed. In the morning light, Pam was still certain they had made the right decision.

The doctor scheduled surgery for the next day and informed Pam that Emily would need six pints of blood instead of the two they had transported.

"We'll give more blood," Pam declared. "We can do that."

"I'm sorry, but there isn't enough time to process it adequately," was the reply. "We'll use your two pints first, and then we'll have to use blood from the hospital supply."

Pam felt no peace about that possibility, so she did what she had done almost continually since the drama began to unfold—she prayed.

"Lord, take care of this problem with the blood. Keep Emily safe from any contaminated blood."

Giving Emily to the surgeon the next day was one of the hardest things Pam and Steve had ever had to do. Early in the morning, the family gathered around her crib, prayed, and sang, "God Is So Good" and "Jesus Loves Me." Then off she went for a possible six hours of surgery.

"I realized I might never see Emily alive again," Pam said. "The next few hours were tough."

*　　　*　　　*

There is no greater love than the love that holds on where there seems nothing left to hold on to.

G. W. C. Thomas

*　　　*　　　*

In four hours the surgery was complete and Emily was still alive.

"When we got to the tumor, we discovered that it was not

vascular. Well, actually, it had been vascular, but all the vessels going to it had dried up," the doctor explained in amazement.

Pam was ecstatic. This was an almost unbelievable answer to prayer! Emily had survived the surgery! The somber look on the surgeon's face, however, warned Pam there was more to report.

"We got all of the tumor we could see with the naked eye," he reported. "I am certain we did not get it all. We sent the mass for a biopsy. Our next step is to wait for the results."

He was done. Those were the facts. But before he left, Pam stopped him. "Oh, by the way," she asked, "how much blood did you use?"

"We used one and a half pints," he replied.

Pam could not contain herself and blurted out, "Isn't that just like God!"

As negative as the doctor had been and as difficult as it was for Emily's family to wait for the biopsy, they still had reason for celebration. They decorated Emily's hospital room with posters, saying, "*God* loves Emily" and "We love Emily." They taped cards and Scripture verses all over the walls. One special verse was taped to Emily's headboard. It was Jeremiah 29:11: "'For I know the plans I have for you,' declares the Lord, 'plans to prosper you and not to harm you, plans to give you hope and a future.'"

After Emily was back in her room, the anesthesiologist came to check on her. The cheerfulness of the room and the proliferation of Bible verses obviously pleased him.

"I can see you are Christians," he declared to Emily's family. "I prayed for your baby throughout the surgery."

How amazing! God had answered unspoken prayers. He had provided Emily with a prayer warrior even in the operating room. That was a blessing that had not even been requested.

Within five days, the biopsy report was in. The tumor was definitely malignant, and Emily would have to undergo chemotherapy immediately.

*　　　*　　　*

If you look at the world, you'll be distressed.

If you look within, you'll be depressed.

If you look at God, you'll be at rest.

Corrie ten Boom

*　　　*　　　*

"We don't rate cancer anymore from stage one to stage four," their surgeon explained, "but if we did, this would be off the scale. She will have to have chemotherapy for at least two years to prolong her life until she can have radiation."

This was another bleak report—but not bleak enough to extinguish Pam's hope. Emily's treatment began the next week. She was on a rigorous schedule of chemotherapy followed by a rest and then chemotherapy again. This regimen was to last for two years. Every three months Emily spent several days in the hospital, undergoing tests. Pam added an important request to her prayer list.

"Each time we went into the hospital," Pam explained, "I asked the Lord to send Emily the perfect roommate. I wanted someone to whom I could witness and for whom I could pray. God answered that prayer time and again."

One of Emily's roommates was a little boy with leukemia. Pam tried to share the encouragement of Christ with this young boy and his family.

"I prayed for openings to lift up Jesus," Pam said. "God's Word is so clear; it says that if we lift Him up, He will draw men to Himself" (see John 12:32). "I didn't have to do any convincing or coercing; I just had to lift up Jesus."

The little boy's mother knew that Pam prayed for Emily, for her little boy, and for many others, including the doctors and nurses. At one point she told a friend, "Ask Pam to pray for you. She has a hotline to God." She didn't say it maliciously or mockingly; she truly believed that somehow Pam had an inside track to God.

"Her comment gave me the perfect opportunity to tell her that she could have the same access to God through Jesus. God's not finished working in her life yet." And neither is Pam. They are still in contact and get together once a year. Pam's prayer is that one day this woman will establish a relationship with Jesus Christ.

*   *   *

For I know whom I have believed, and am persuaded

that he is able to keep that which I have

committed unto him against that day.

2 Timothy 1:12 KJV

*   *   *

Chemotherapy continued for the next two years. There were ups and downs and challenges, both physically and emotionally.

"After you've been in a fight like this for an extended length of time," Pam explained, "you begin to feel you're the Lone Ranger. Other people get on with their lives, but you don't. You have to keep repeating painful scenarios."

At one point Pam was especially drained. The chemotherapy schedule had been a wearying one, and one day she felt that her stamina was gone.

She cried out to God, "Lord, I can go through anything with You, but I want to do something for You. If You could give me someone to witness to, I would be so grateful. You see, I would like to call it quits right now and never take Emily back for chemotherapy again. But if You can give me somebody to whom I can show Your love, I know I can go on."

Two days later, it was time once again for Emily's treatment. The clinic was especially crowded that day. After a short while, a young woman came out of one of the treatment rooms. She had a three- or four-year-old in tow and was probably nine months pregnant. As she made her way through the waiting room, she was sobbing.

*　　*　　*

God has said,
"Never will I leave you;
never will I forsake you."
Hebrews 13:5b

*　　*　　*

"When I looked at her, I knew she was the one God wanted me to help," Pam said. "So I grabbed a box of tissues and took them to her, and we became the best of friends. In the next year I spent hours with her on the phone."

This new friend asked Pam hard questions: "Why do I have a sick child? How could God do this to my baby?"

"I didn't know the answers to many of her questions. But I told her what I did know: that God loved her and her little boy and that God was willing to give them both a future and a hope through Jesus," Pam said. "None of us knows how long we'll live, but that future and hope will eventually mean a place in heaven. There is no better hope."

*　　*　　*

I have held many things in my hands
and have lost them all;
But the things I have placed in God's hands,
those I always possess.
Earline Steelburg

*　　*　　*

Emily finished chemotherapy, and the doctors declared that, miraculously, she did not need radiation. This was atypical. With Emily's type of cancer these two treatments usually went hand in hand. God had answered another prayer.

Several years have passed now, and Emily has had no recurrence of the cancer. She is a beautiful thirteen-year-old child whose life is a testimony to the amazing power of prayer.

"I don't know why God chose Emily," Pam said tearfully. "I will never know why. I just know that His ways are not our ways."

*   *   *

"For my thoughts are not your thoughts,

neither are your ways my ways," declares the Lord.

Isaiah 55:8

*   *   *

For years Emily, Pam, and the rest of the family have volunteered three or four times a year to be houseparents at the Ronald McDonald House. That is where they stayed each time Emily was hospitalized.

"When we are there I tell Emily's story," Pam said. "It's a story of hope and prayer and faith. Some families are obviously receptive, and some are not. I gently tell the story to everyone. And if they want prayer, I pray."

Pam always asks God to help her focus on one family. She adds that family to her prayer list and encourages them with notes of love for the next few months. After one visit, she added Sam to her prayer list. Sam had undergone a stem-cell rescue and was suffering from septic shock. His body was greatly damaged. He was on a respirator and the medical prognosis was bleak.

"I had been praying for Sam and his family for months. The next time we visited the Ronald McDonald House, I was able to ask an oncology nurse about his progress," Pam said.

"Pam," she replied, "you don't understand. There can be no progress. He is on a respirator and they are waiting for him to die. There is no hope."

"There is always hope. I believe in miracles," Pam said in response.

"You are not being realistic," the nurse said.

Thus the conversation ended. But Pam's prayers did not. She continued praying for Sam, asking God for a miracle.

The next week Pam's phone rang. It was the oncology nurse.

"Sam just went home," the nurse began. "He has a tracheotomy, but he is off of the respirator. I knew you'd want to know. I can't believe it."

"You will someday," Pam replied. "I know you will someday."

Pam chose to pray. She chose to pray not only for the urgent circumstances surrounding Emily's illness but for others too. At any point in her journey she could have fallen into the rut of choosing the "if onlys." If only Emily had not developed a tumor, Pam might have had the time to be a prayer warrior for others. If only Emily had not had to have chemotherapy, Pam might have been able to minister to others. But Pam's choice to bring the needs of others before God's throne disarmed the "if onlys" and led to great blessings.

*   *   *

Daily prayers will diminish your cares.

Betty Mills

*   *   *

CHOOSE TO
Reflect

Jesus, God's own Son, was faithful in prayer. He chose to be in fellowship with His heavenly Father. God desires that we do the same. His Word says we can "approach the throne of grace with confidence" (Hebrews 4:16). How wonderful to know we are welcomed by our heavenly Father.

STUDY QUESTIONS

Choose to Pray

1. Read James 5:13–18. Have you ever seen a miraculous answer to prayer?

2. How can you develop perseverance in prayer? Do you know someone who is a faithful prayer warrior? Consider asking that person to join you for lunch so you can learn how he or she developed and maintained the discipline of prayer.

3. How can you set aside time daily to pray for others? How might the use of a prayer journal help you?

4. Who might be a regular prayer warrior for you? Who might be a prayer partner with you?

4

CHOOSE JOY

*The highest pinnacle of the spiritual life
is not joy in unbroken sunshine
but absolute and undoubting trust
in the love of God.*

W. THOROLD

It was Shirley's forty-seventh birthday, a day not unlike other days in Shirley's life. It was filled with activities and events. She had to renew her driver's license, attend a church meeting, and squeeze in jury duty. As Shirley showered to begin her busy day, she felt a lump in her breast. Well, that certainly didn't fit into her schedule. Maybe she'd have time to call her doctor today, if she finished her errands soon enough. Later in the afternoon she found the time to call.

"Dr. Clancy?" Shirley inquired. "I hate to bother you, but I figured I should call. When I was showering this morning, I felt a lump in my breast."

"It's probably just a clogged milk duct," he reassured her. "Come in tomorrow and have a mammogram. If it doesn't show anything, we'll wait for a month. If it's still there after that time, give me a call."

This timetable fit Shirley just fine. She went in the next day for the mammogram. It didn't show any abnormalities, so she put the lump out of her mind until several weeks later, after the Christmas holidays. The pesky lump was still there. She called her doctor again, and he scheduled a biopsy. As she prepared for the scheduled surgery, a nurse brought in some paperwork.

"We need you to sign this," the nurse told Shirley. "It says that if deemed necessary the physician can do a mastectomy."

"Whew," Shirley exclaimed. "We have now gone from a clogged milk duct to a possible mastectomy. That was incredibly fast!"

As Shirley reached the operating room, she questioned the nurses about how long she would be in surgery. Their reply was twenty to forty minutes for a biopsy, two hours for a mastectomy. It was 11:45 a.m. The next thing Shirley was aware of was someone calling her name and trying to rouse her. She opened her eyes. The clock on the wall read 2:00 p.m. Shirley knew the outcome of the surgery.

Things change. Life is not guaranteed in longevity or in quality. Shirley experienced a tremendous change that day. She faced a serious disease—a killer—eyeball to eyeball. Two months before the surgery, Shirley had claimed to be in top condition; now her prognosis was listed as poor. Her health status had changed drastically and officially in a little over two hours. She had no control over her circumstances, but she did have a choice about her attitude.

In the face of this unfolding drama, Shirley could have chosen to play the "what if" game. "What if I never see my kids graduate from high school?" "What if it's even worse than the doctors think?" "What if I can never have a normal day again?"

"What if I don't make it until next Christmas?"

The "what if" game is a game that has no winner. It is a little like the "if only" exercise.

"If only this hadn't happened to me, I might have been able to do something for Christ. I might have been able to make a difference in someone's life."

"If only I didn't have cancer, I could be joyful."

Shirley could play "what if" or "if only," or she could keep her attitude joyful. The choice was hers to make.

Shirley was scheduled for chemotherapy, and she prepared for it by reading all she could find on the procedure. Each brochure and pamphlet listed possible side effects: "You may experience nausea, fatigue, loss of appetite." And each piece of literature said, "You will experience the loss of your hair."

The use of the words *may experience* helped Shirley to imagine that she could dodge the majority of the chemotherapy symptoms. But the statement "You *will* experience the loss of your hair" really bothered her.

On the recommendation of her oncologist, Shirley called Jan, a woman who had undergone two mastectomies and was trained as a counselor for women in similar situations. Shirley told Jan about her difficulty accepting the fact that she would lose her hair.

"I know what you mean," Jan replied. "That was the hardest thing for me too. It was so terrible."

"Oh, great," Shirley thought. "The last thing I need is someone who is all gloom and doom. Jan said it was terrible. I don't need to hear about terrible."

Then Jan continued. "In fact," she said, "I told my husband I didn't mind putting my boob in the drawer at night but I didn't want to hang my hair on the doorknob."

Shirley laughed out loud. The picture Jan had painted with her words was like a funny cartoon. Jan gave Shirley a tremendous gift that day. She reminded Shirley that despite the circumstances, she could choose joy and laughter. And that is precisely what Shirley did. Shirley chose to face her situation with joy and to look for opportunities to laugh and to share joy and laughter with others.

On one of Shirley's visits to her oncologist soon after her surgery, he personally discovered her choice for joy. At that time he informed her that the cancer had not been limited to the breast tissue but instead it was also located in the lymph nodes. He explained that this created a much more serious problem.

"We do have some good news though," Shirley's doctor said. "We can give you a drug that will eliminate the estrogen in your body. The estrogen is feeding the cancer."

"What will that mean?" Shirley asked.

"You will immediately enter menopause. You will have hot flashes, become irritable, and the aging process will be accelerated greatly," Shirley's doctor replied.

Shirley looked him straight in the eye and repeated the symptoms: "Immediate menopause. Hot flashes. Irritability and accelerated aging. Please tell me again," she said, with a smirk. "This is the good news?" Even her doctor had to chuckle as he realized the irony. They determined that good news was definitely a relative matter.

*   *   *

Consider it pure joy, my brothers,
whenever you face trials of many kinds.
James 1:2

*   *   *

Chemotherapy itself gave Shirley an opportunity to be joyful and to influence others with her attitude. She knew that some women arrived for chemotherapy with no smile, with no makeup, and surrounded by a dark cloud of gloom. She decided to take the opposite approach. For each session she dressed in something bright and cheerful. She made sure her wig (yes, her hair did fall out) was done well, and she wore big, dangly earrings. Equally important was the smile she wore to chemotherapy. Shirley chose joy.

Several months after Shirley finished chemotherapy, I heard her give a devotional at a convention. Few people in the audience knew Shirley, and even fewer knew of her circumstances. Her message that day was on the sovereignty of God.

"About twenty years ago I gave a devotional at a women's group. Then I declared, 'Nothing has ever gone wrong in my life because God is in control. He is a sovereign God.' After that message, women in their forties and beyond tried to help me out a little," Shirley explained. "'You're just young. Wait until you have a little more maturity. Wait till you've lived a few more years.' Okay," Shirley continued, "today I'm in my late forties, and I stand before you to say nothing has ever gone wrong in my life because God is in control. He's a sovereign God. That does not mean that Satan is not scheming and making his best attempt to kill, steal, and destroy. But he is the enemy, and I am on the winning side. Nothing bad has ever happened in my life."

Nothing bad—just a radical mastectomy and chemotherapy. Those were merely circumstances that could only affect Shirley's temporary happiness. She did not allow them to affect her joy.

There's a difference between joy and happiness. Happiness is based on happenings. Joy is an inside job. It's a fruit of the Holy Spirit. Shirley chose joy.

*　　*　　*

Laughter is a tranquilizer with no side effects.
Arnold H. Glasow

*　　*　　*

"You know you're in trouble when the 'best if used by' date on your donor's card has expired," Shirley quipped and then laughed enthusiastically as though she'd just heard the joke for the first time.

I laughed, too, because it was funny and she was funny. I was always refreshed in her presence. Several years ago, Shirley and I were attending a surprisingly somber and boring conference when to our amazement we found ourselves plotting a mutiny—a takeover of the stage, the microphone, and ultimately (we hoped) the mood of the conference. We found three other willing participants and developed our plan.

Right at the point when the emcee dismissed the group for the morning break, we cued the soundman to begin our tape. The Amy Grant recording blared out the song "Fat Baby," at which point we emerged from behind the curtain as Amy, backup singers ("Wah, Wah, Wah"), and two grown men dressed in shorts, t-shirts, and dorm bedsheet diapers.

The plan went off without a hitch. The audience went wild. The laughter was uproarious. And the great success of the stunt somehow even landed us in the good graces of the conference leaders. I guess they needed a good laugh too.

What a risk we took, all for joy and laughter. Emerson once said, "Laugh often, laugh much." Shirley knew the power of laughter in those relatively carefree years and knew its power again when calamity could have been king.

Shirley is not alone in the realization of the power of laughter and joy. The most influential catalyst thrusting laughter to a place of prominence as a positive influence on people and their health was probably Norman Cousins. Cousins prescribed laughter for himself. "He got relief from pain from a degenerative disease when he guffawed his way through humorous videos."[2]

Today researchers can explain the positive effects of laughter and a joyful outlook. "After you laugh, you go into a relaxed state," explains John Morreall, PhD, president of HUMOR-WORKS Seminars in Tampa, Florida. "Your blood pressure and heart rate drop below normal, you feel profoundly relaxed.

Laughter also indirectly stimulates endorphins, the brain's natural painkillers."[3] A Loma Linda University study showed that "thirty minutes after twenty medical students laughed through a video of a well-known comedian, their disease-fighting white blood cells increased by 25 percent."[4]

Norman Cousins had to leave the hospital to view the humorous, health-enhancing videos. Now it is possible to receive a dose of laughter without checking out of the hospital. There are now hospitals with clown schools on site, humor carts, and imported clowns.[5]

The truth of the positive power of choosing joy and laughter is not new. God's Word is filled with statements verifying the fact:

- A cheerful heart is good medicine (Proverbs 17:22).
- A happy heart makes the face cheerful (Proverbs 15:13).
- A cheerful look brings joy to the heart. . . . The cheerful heart has a continual feast (Proverbs 15:30, 15).
- The joy of the Lord is your strength (Nehemiah 8:10).

Why, it has even been suggested that God has a sense of humor. Think of the duck-billed platypus and the aardvark, two of God's humorous creations. Consider God's plagues against the Egyptians. They were ingenious and some were almost funny. Envision Jesus talking about taking the speck out of your brother's eye while there is a log in yours. That's a funny picture.[6]

All of this adds up to a great deal of support for the choice of joy. And yet sometimes we fail to choose joy. What can keep us from this choice? What things did Shirley have to combat in order to choose joy?

She told me once that besides Satan, whose number one mission, as we read in John 10:10, is to steal, kill, and destroy, there are other potential robbers of joy. The general attitude of society is one great big joy robber. Think about it. The evening news is usually pretty depressing. The world, it would seem, is going to hell in a handbasket. Any evening, in just thirty minutes you can relive murders, robberies, social injustices, blight, and numerous natural disasters. Pretty depressing, huh?

Then there's the weather. Tomorrow we have a 10 percent chance of rain. (Oh, no! My cookout will be ruined.) Wait a minute! A 10 percent chance of rain means a 90 percent chance of sunshine. (I won't cancel the cookout after all.) The negative attitude of our society can rob us of our joy.

Stress is another deterrent to joy. We used to think of young business executives as the only ones living stressful lives. Now we hear that stress is a leading negative in the lives of teenagers.

Shirley once gave me a copy of a stress diet that she had discovered. Here it is:

Stress Diet

BREAKFAST:

1/2 grapefruit

1 slice whole wheat bread

8 oz. skim milk

LUNCH:

4 oz. lean broiled chicken

1 c. steamed zucchini

1 Oreo cookie

Herb tea

AFTERNOON SNACK:

Remainder of Oreo package

1 qt. Rocky Road ice cream

1 jar hot fudge

DINNER:

2 loaves garlic bread

Large pepperoni pizza

2 Milky Way candy bars

Whole frozen cheesecake,

eaten directly from freezer

Helpful Hints:

- If no one sees you eat it, it has no calories.
- If you drink a diet soda with a candy bar, they cancel each other out.
- When eating with someone else, there is no need to count calories if you both eat the same amount.
- Food taken for medicinal purposes, such as hot chocolate, toast, and Sara Lee cheesecake, never counts.
- If you fatten up those around you, you will look thinner.

I'm not sure that the diet relieved my stress, but the laughter it evoked made a difference.

Negative people can also rob us of our joy. Attitudes are contagious. When Shirley's white count was down after chemotherapy, she avoided people with colds and the flu. Regardless of her blood count status, however, she avoided people with negative attitudes.

Shirley told me once that fear was another joy robber. One weekend about six months after her cancer was discovered, Shirley started vomiting. Ultimately she was so dehydrated that her husband had to take her to the emergency room of a local hospital. After the attending physician examined her and asked her many questions about the medications she had been taking, he asked her a question followed by a statement that instantly produced fear in Shirley's mind.

"Have you had a brain scan recently?" the emergency doctor inquired. "I think the cancer has gone to your brain."

Shirley reacted not only with fear but also with anger: "I'm going to let my oncologist do all the diagnosing of cancer. Thank you very much."

The doctor didn't press his diagnosis, but his guess had done its temporary damage. Shirley told me that from the moment of his careless statement until the next Tuesday, when she could finally visit her oncologist, she was plagued with fear. The visit on Tuesday with her cancer doctor was very positive. She did not have a brain tumor. It was then that Shirley realized that fear had successfully stolen her joy for several days.

"Do you know what fear is?" Shirley asked me once. "It is:

F – alse
E – vidence
A – ppearing
R – eal

When we realize that, we've stripped fear of its power." That definition went a long way toward restoring Shirley's joy.

I remember Shirley telling me about a get-together for a friend before his surgery. It was estimated that he had a 5 percent chance of survival. As the evening and the party unfolded, Shirley realized she really didn't know too much about the circumstances of the illness, the surgery, or the 5 percent chance. She decided that there was no time like the present to ask some questions.

"So you're scheduled for surgery on Thursday, right?" Shirley asked the upcoming patient.

"That's right," he replied.

"I hear you have a 5 percent chance. What exactly does that mean?"

"The doctor says I have a 5 percent chance of having a heart attack in recovery from my gall bladder surgery," he said gloomily.

"A 5 percent chance of a heart attack?" Shirley howled. "That means a 95 percent chance of no heart attack. Those are terrific odds!"

The man paused and then seemed to understand the math for the very first time. A smile came across his face, followed by a smirk, and then a belly laugh. Before long the other guests were wondering what could possibly be so amusing that Shirley and the guest of honor were laughing to the point of tears.

*   *   *

**Joy is the holy fire that keeps our
purpose warm and our intelligence aglow.**
Helen Keller

*   *   *

From the outset, Shirley's prognosis was listed on her medical records as poor. After five years of joyfully fighting the disease and testing cancer free, Shirley asked her physician if he could upgrade her prognosis. On her prodding, he finally changed the record from "prognosis—poor" to "prognosis—guarded."

"This is an upgrade?" she asked jokingly. And then she accepted her victory, be it ever so small.

I have heard people say that, at best, life is terminal. That is true. After seven and a half years, Shirley faced two more rounds of chemotherapy, one round of radiation, and many doses of powerful medication. As we ate lunch together one day, after all these medical procedures, I asked Shirley if she ever asked the physicians what her life expectancy was.

"I don't bother to ask the doctors," she replied. "What do they know for sure? Besides, I just signed the paperwork for a fifteen-year mortgage on our new house."

*   *   *

Until further notice, celebrate everything.
David Wolfe

*   *   *

Later that day I heard her tell the story of the two sisters who faithfully ate oat bran and lived long and healthy lives. Ultimately these two women died and went to be with Jesus in glory. One sister was practically speechless over the beauty and awesomeness of heaven. The other sister seemed to be pouting. When the first sister finally realized that she was alone in her excitement, she asked the pouting sister why.

"Well," said the sober sister, "if you hadn't made me eat all that oat bran, I could have been here sooner."

Shirley laughed, actually before the punch line, and I laughed too. It was funny, Shirley was funny, and her joy was contagious.

A joyful person—one choosing joy in spite of the circumstances—is one who celebrates life and embraces its abundance. So on that day, Shirley and I ate lunch together and celebrated our friendship. We celebrated life and its fragility. We celebrated joy. And we celebrated the sovereignty of God. Shirley had chosen joy, and she was empowered by that choice.

*   *   *

The most wasted of all our days are
those in which we have not laughed.
Sebastian Chamfort

*   *   *

CHOOSE TO
Reflect

It is possible to face our trials with joy. The key lies in realizing that our joy is not based on our circumstances. The trials you face today may or may not be the trials of yesterday or of tomorrow. Trials change . . . circumstances change . . . God does not change. "Jesus Christ is the same yesterday and today and forever" (Hebrews 13:8).

STUDY QUESTIONS

Choose Joy

1. Read James 1:2–4. What do you learn from James about trials?
2. What trial have you faced recently? Were you able to find joy in the midst of that trial? Why or why not?
3. Scientific research and God's Word both indicate that laughter is good medicine. Have you personally experienced the positive power of laughter?
4. Can you share a time when FEAR (False Evidence Appearing Real) stole your joy? Has anything else been able to rob you of your joy?

5

CHOOSE NOT TO WORRY

Cast all your anxiety on him
because he cares for you.

1 PETER 5:7

Betty didn't get smacked around every day—just often enough to keep her jumpy. The frequency of Pete's hitting her was unpredictable.

"There was nothing I could do to avoid provoking Pete," she said. "There was no logic, no formula. What made him mad one day didn't bother him the next. Something that didn't faze him today might send him into a rage tomorrow."

It took Betty many years to realize that her husband's explosions could not be eliminated by anything she did or didn't do. The unpredictability of his angry attacks kept her off balance and kept Pete in control of her life.

"He would throw me against the wall, or down the stairs, or into furniture when he was angry," Betty explained. "And he would swing at me, connecting with my face most of the time. I remember wishing he'd break my jaw, so that I would have to go to the doctor."

At the same time she wanted to see a doctor, she was also reluctant to see one. Part of the ploy of an abusive husband is to convince his wife that the abuse is *her* fault. He leads her to believe that she has caused the lashing out, that she has done something to "deserve" the beatings. This makes it difficult for the woman to seek help, lest her helpers also tell her she's to blame.

Logic and sound thinking tell us that this line of reasoning is absurd. What could anyone do to "deserve" being hit by another person? Logic, however, is not part of an abusive relationship.

"We had a very unreliable car, and it invariably acted up when I had it on the road," Betty said. "One day I stopped at the grocery store and it refused to start. I cranked the ignition key and tried every trick I could think of to get it started. Finally I had no choice except to call Pete. He arrived and fiddled under the hood until the car started. Then I followed him home."

The scene that followed was terrifying. When she drove up, Pete pulled her from the car and shoved her into the garage.

"Why couldn't you get the *&*% car started?" he shrieked. "You are so *%$ stupid! I'm going to beat some sense into you so this doesn't happen again."

He pushed and struck her but quickly got bored with the one-sided fight. In frustration he walked to his truck and roared out of the driveway.

Betty lay crumpled in a back corner of the garage. The blows Pete had landed had not been as bad as usual, but Betty's spirit was broken. She thought long and hard about the possibility that Pete might kill her during one of these beatings. It was a thought she had lived with for several years. Who would care for their children if she were gone?

Twelve years before, when this young couple had been

dating, Betty hadn't noticed any short fuse or abusive behavior in Pete. Maybe she had been blinded by infatuation or by Pete's dashing good looks. Her parents had had some reservations about him, but they had been reassured when Betty told them that Pete had said he was a Christian.

"My mistake was listening to his talk and not watching his walk," she said, years later. "I heard what I wanted to hear, and I hid my eyes from the signs that he was lying when he said he was a Christian."

After they were married, Betty discovered that Pete had no desire to be involved in a church and no intention of worshiping with her on Sunday mornings. In fact, he attempted to sabotage Betty's efforts to attend church.

"Pete wanted to go to bars and party on Saturday night. He would get angry with me when I went along because I didn't want to drink," Betty explained. "And he'd get just as angry if I stayed home. He absolutely refused to get up for church the next morning, and he did everything he could to get me to stay home too."

It did not take long for Betty to realize that Pete had married her under false pretenses. Pete was not a Christian. In fact, he seemed to loathe the church and people who had accepted Christ.

"At first I worried a great deal about his salvation," Betty said. "What could I do to bring him to Christ? What could I say?" But the more Betty attempted to say and do the perfect thing to lead Pete to a saving knowledge of Christ, the more Pete seemed to reject the Lord.

"At one point, I realized that my worry was not accomplishing a thing. I could not worry Pete into heaven, nor could I push him in. My responsibility was to live in a Christ-like manner before him. So," she continued, "I chose to give him to God. I had to quit worrying."

∗   ∗   ∗

Don't worry about anything; instead, pray about everything.
Tell God what you need, and thank him for all he has done.
Then you will experience God's peace,
which exceeds anything we can understand.

Philippians 4:6–7 NLT

∗   ∗   ∗

Although Betty chose to stop worrying about Pete's relationship with Christ (or lack of it), she was rapidly making other disturbing discoveries about her new husband.

"Within months of our wedding, I became pregnant. I was momentarily taken aback. 'We're already off to a rocky start,' I thought. 'How will I handle this added responsibility?'"

She discovered all too soon how Pete would react to his new and increased responsibility. It was when she was pregnant with Jessica, their older daughter, that Pete first became violent. He came home late one night after spending the evening in the bars. Betty wondered where he had been and she met him at the door.

"I'm so glad you're home," she said. "Did you have car trouble?"

"No, I didn't have *any* trouble," Pete said angrily. "And it's none of your business if I did. I don't need to report in to you all the time. You're not my mother!"

With that he struck her in the face with the back of his hand and marched into the house. The blow caused Betty to stumble backward. Her cheek was stinging, and her heart was broken.

How could her husband hit her? What if she had tripped and fallen? What if the baby had been hurt? The incident left her questioning what her future was to be.

By morning Betty had made a decision. She could not live with a man who hit her. And she could not bring a new baby into a violent household. She packed up her essentials and left Pete, returning to her parents' home in a nearby community.

Pete did not realize what had happened until he came home from work late that afternoon. When he discovered Betty was gone, he made a quick phone call to her parents' home.

"Is Betty there?" he asked.

"She is," her dad replied, "but she is not interested in speaking to you."

"What's going on? I don't understand. If it's about last night, well, I can explain that. I had a little too much to drink and when Betty met me at the door, she startled me. I didn't mean to hurt her. I would never hurt her. I am so sorry. Please forgive me," he pleaded. "Nothing like this will ever happen again. Please, please let me talk to Betty and tell her how sorry I am." They talked, and Betty went home.

Saying "I'm sorry" is easy. Meaning it and having a repentant heart and a change in behavior are more difficult. Pete's "I'm sorry" was meaningless, as Betty would soon discover.

After little Jessica was born, the abusive behavior surfaced again. With a baby in the house, Betty thought it might be nice to have a second car. Pete wasn't always easy to catch at work, and she hated having to depend on a neighbor if Jessica needed to go to the doctor. It would also be nice to shop for groceries during the day, she thought, instead of waiting until Pete got home in the evening.

A young man Betty and Pete knew had a car with a For Sale sign on it. Betty suggested they drive over and take a look at it. The battle didn't begin until after they returned home.

"Did you like the car?" Betty asked.

"I thought it was overpriced," Pete replied.

"Oh, I don't know," continued Betty. "He said it had four new tires and had recently had a tune-up."

"I don't know why you should trust him," Pete growled back. "Do you think he knows more about cars than I do?"

"I didn't say that," Betty replied. "I just thought it was a nice car."

"I don't care what you think," Pete yelled. By now he was visibly angry. "You don't know anything, anyway!"

"Fine, let's just drop it," Betty suggested. "We don't need to get that car."

"No, I'm not going to drop it! If you think you know more about cars than I do, you can just get out of here and get yourself a car," Pete exploded.

By now there was no stopping Pete's anger, and nothing that Betty could say or do would soothe him. He reached across the table and grabbed her arm. Even though she yelled at him to stop, he jerked her out of the chair and literally dragged her across the kitchen floor. When he got to the back door, he opened it and pushed her into the yard with all his strength. Betty lay in the backyard, sobbing and struggling to grasp what had happened.

This time Betty did not go to her parents' home. In her confused state of mind she thought she had used up her second chances. Now she would have to stick it out and make the best of the situation. And unbeknownst to Pete or to her folks, Betty was pregnant again.

*   *   *

The Lord shall preserve thy going out
and thy coming in from this time forth,
and even forevermore.
Psalm 121:8 KJV

*   *   *

Those of us in healthy marriages have a difficult time understanding what holds a woman in an abusive relationship such as Betty's. We don't understand the *despair* that binds a woman's hands against action. The abuser convinces his spouse that there is no hope and that no one can help her. The result is unremitting despair.

Guilt is another binding force. The victim is brainwashed into believing *she* is responsible for the abuser's violent actions.

Pride can also hold an abused woman in a frightening situation. She does not want to admit that she has chosen a mate so poorly.

Fear and *worry* about life, limb, family, and future also trap the abused woman. How will she survive financially?

Betty was a Christian, and she felt certain that with God's help she would be able to build a marriage. She didn't think that divorce was an option.

*   *   *

I will lift up my eyes to the mountains;

From where shall my help come?

My help comes from the Lord,

who made heaven and earth.

Psalm 121:1–2 NASB

*   *   *

With the arrival of their second child, Sally, Betty became more concerned about the lack of parenting the girls received from Pete. Typically he ignored them or acted as though they were a nuisance. He provided no spiritual guidance or encouragement.

"I remember lying in my bed one night and realizing Pete was not going to be the father that he was supposed to be to the kids. I knew that, and I knew I had to go forward and do what I could to be a good mother to my children. I wanted them to have a Christian home and a church. I realized that, in the spiritual sense, I was responsible for these young lives. I needed to teach them the way of the Lord and bring them the gospel.

That was my responsibility. I also had to understand that I was not responsible for my husband's salvation or his parenting. I said to God, 'I'll be their mother, but You're going to have to be their Father. They don't have a father who will pray with them or read the Bible to them or teach them about You. You are going to have to Father them. I'm not going to worry. I know You will meet their needs.'"

Betty relinquished this worry and responsibility to God. She was not going to be able to control Pete's interaction with the girls by worrying.

*　　　*　　　*

Therefore do not worry about tomorrow,

for tomorrow will worry about itself.

Each day has enough trouble of its own.

Matthew 6:34

*　　　*　　　*

While Betty tried not to worry about Pete's salvation or poor parenting skills, she was worried that someday in a fit of rage Pete might take her life. What if that happened? Who would care for her children?

One day things came to a frightening head for Betty. It had been an exhaustingly combative day. It seemed as though Pete had reacted negatively to every word she had spoken. Even the dinner she served made him angry. It looked as though another explosion was imminent.

Betty was on pins and needles all day. Somehow she was able to avoid any form of major conflict throughout the day, but by nighttime she was exhausted. It was all she could do to finish the dishes, help the kids with their homework, and fall into bed. She had avoided physical attack, but she was exhausted by the verbal attacks Pete had volleyed at her all day.

"Dear Lord," she prayed, "I don't know how much more I can take. Please, Father, do something. I can't go on much longer."

And the still small voice of God spoke to her heart: *It won't be much longer now.*

Betty knew in that instant that God was going to take care of her. She interpreted God's words to mean that her time on earth would be ending before too long. She felt that God was telling her that He had things under control.

Yes, God did have everything under control, but Betty's life on earth was not coming to an end. Instead, her torturous living conditions were soon to change. That night Betty chose not to worry about her own life. She put her trust wholly in God.

*   *   *

Do not be anxious about anything,

but in everything, by prayer and petition,

with thanksgiving, present your requests to God.

Philippians 4:6

*   *   *

Within two weeks Betty's nephew confronted her about the abuse he suspected. When she admitted the severity of her situation, her nephew encouraged her to leave Pete. She left her children with a friend and boarded a plane bound for her parents' new home in another state. In this protective setting, Betty took time to sort through the facts and her feelings. The time away was like a sweet balm. She was able to clear her head and see the futility of continuing her dangerous living situation. From that time on, she never again lived with Pete.

Studies show that an abused woman's safety is most at stake after she leaves her abuser. That fact alone could have caused Betty to worry. And what about a place to live? Her family was not living near her any longer, and she wanted to keep the girls in their own school. She wanted to keep their lives as normal as possible.

Betty chose not to live in her What Ifs. She had a restraining order placed on Pete and tried to be wise about having friends from church escort her and the girls to their school activities. Her church rose to the occasion and helped her find a place to live— first in a friend's extra room, and then in low-income housing. Miraculously, the Lord met Betty's financial needs.

"One day when we came home to the apartment," she said, "we found an envelope had been slipped under the door. It contained seven one-hundred-dollar bills. That was it! No name, no address, no one to thank but God."

Betty chose not to worry but to let God meet their needs. By this time, she had been practicing not worrying with regularity, and it was becoming easier and easier to make the next right choice for her life.

＊　　　＊　　　＊

Worry never robs tomorrow of its sorrow,

it only saps today of its joy.

Leo Buscaglia

＊　　　＊　　　＊

Many of us worry about things that are much less monumental than the troubles Betty had in her life. It's not that we like to worry or that we need to worry. More than anything, worry is a habit. We choose to live in the What Ifs of life.

"It's only natural to worry," you say. "After all, Kendra, I come from a rich heritage of worriers. My mother worried, my grandmother worried, and her mother before her. It's genetic. All the women in my family worry."

Nice try, but I really don't think worry is genetic. I think it's a choice. The problem is that we have been trained and conditioned to worry, and worrying has become our natural response to many situations.

I was eating dinner one day with a large group of friends. Something was obviously bothering the young woman sitting next to me. As we were being served dessert, she finally addressed the issue that had been on her mind.

"Kendra, I want to talk to you about something," she began.

"Sure," I replied, and encouraged her to go on.

"I am worried about something," she continued. "I am worried about my kids."

I did a quick mental inventory and realized there was seemingly nothing to worry about when it came to her kids. She had two healthy, happy boys who were well behaved and achieving well in school.

"Have I missed something?" I asked. "Is there something wrong with one of the boys? Is there a problem at school or at home?"

"Well," she hesitated, "no, there isn't anything in particular. I just worry about them."

"You have great kids; there is no need to worry," I reassured her.

"There's something else. I worry about my husband," she said sheepishly.

Again I racked my brain to see if I could identify what might be motivating this particular worry. Again I came up blank.

"Why are you worrying about your husband? He's healthy. He loves you and is a good father and provider. Do you really have any reason to worry about him?" I asked.

"No, I guess not," she sighed. "Oh, I also worry about plane crashes."

"Do you have any airplane tickets? Do you know anyone who has ever been in a plane crash?" I questioned as patiently as possible.

"No," she said with a hint of embarrassment. "But, Kendra, there is one more thing."

"Go ahead," I said, wondering where we were going from here.

"I worry that maybe I worry too much," she blurted out.

"Now, I just might agree with you on that one," I said, laughing.

*   *   *

Blessed is the person who is too busy to worry

in the daytime and too sleepy to worry at night.

Leo Aikman

*   *   *

Worry can be consuming. I once heard it said that "worry time" is wasted time. So choosing not to worry is a positive, empowering choice. How can we do it?

I learned an important lesson long ago at a Little League park. All three of my boys played Little League baseball. When our eldest son was about ten years old, he went into the game one night as a relief pitcher. Now, just in case some of you are unfamiliar with Little League, let me help you out. These are little boys—eight, nine, and ten years old. The role of the pitcher is paramount because it is very seldom that one of the boys hits the ball. If the pitcher pitches strikes, the batters typically strike out. If he pitches balls, the bases fill up mighty quick. You see, runs are scored not so much by making hits but by loading the bases with walks.

On this particular night, the bases were downright crowded when Matthew went in to pitch. You can imagine the kind of night the previous pitcher had been having, to load up the bases. Matthew took his spot on the mound, wound up, and threw the ball.

"Ball one," the umpire shouted.

My motherly instincts and my overwhelming urge to help overtook my brain and I yelled some constructive words to Matthew.

"Pitch a strike, Matthew," I bellowed from the stands. The wind up . . . the pitch . . .

"Ball two," the umpire countered.

Obviously Matthew had not heard me. So this time I yelled even louder.

"PITCH A STRIKE, Matthew," I cried.

"Ball three," said the umpire.

Maybe if I said it slower, it would help.

"P-I-T-C-H A S-T-R-I-K-E, Matthew," I howled.

To tell you the honest truth, I don't remember if that next pitch was a ball or a strike. I vaguely recall that Matthew did provide relief and his team won the game. I do vividly remember, however, our conversation after the game.

"Mom," Matthew began, "I really don't mind if you cheer at ball games. (What a relief! I am a cheerfully vocal fan.) But please don't ever yell, 'Pitch a strike.' Because you see, Mom, if there is anyone in the whole ball field who wants to pitch a strike, it is me! I understand the goal."

Now, I am not a slow learner. I got his message, and his brothers after him benefited greatly from the lesson I learned that evening. So I won't tell you. . . .

"Stop worrying!!"

"STOP WORRYING!!"

"S-T-O-P W-O-R-R-Y-I-N-G!!" You probably already want to do that. Instead, let's see if I can give you some suggestions to help you stop worrying.

One of the truths that has helped me is to realize that *worry consumes priceless, irreplaceable energy.* Typically, my worry list pops into view after I've fallen asleep for the night. Maybe I'm unique in this, but more times than not, I can make it through the day just fine with no time spent in worry. Then give me three or four hours of good sleep, and my brain seems to suddenly turn back on and focus in on a list of worries. This list may contain significant issues or extremely trivial ones, but either way it wakes me up and keeps me awake for varying amounts of time. In the morning, the issues—big or small—are still there, and I am exhausted. Worry has accomplished nothing except to rob me of precious rest. Don't waste energy in worry.

Another key to help you "pitch a strike" and stop worrying is to remember that *worry is a lack of faith.* "Therefore I tell you, do not worry about your life, what you will eat or drink; or about your body, what you will wear. Is not life more than food, and the body more than clothes? Look at the birds of the air; they do not sow or reap or store away in barns, and yet your heavenly Father feeds them. Are you not much more valuable than they? Can any one of you by worrying add a single hour to your life?" (Matthew 6:25–27). Either we believe God is in control or we do not.

This leads me to my third suggestion. Why do we think that life would be better if we were in control? We worry that things won't go the way we planned. But who says our plans are the best? We worry when we are unable to move all the chess pieces of life to the squares we have chosen for them. In order to stop worrying, *we must release control of our lives to God.*

*   *   *

Worrying is like a rocking chair:

It gives you something to do but doesn't get you anywhere.

Glenn Turner

*   *   *

Finally, let me present an age-old remedy for worry. It is called preparation. How many times do we worry about the things for which we have failed to prepare? Ask any student who has failed to study if he is worried. Preparation can replace worry.

Several months ago I had a Pap test with worrisome results. My physician recommended that I visit a specialist. I was able to get an appointment within two weeks and met with my new doctor.

"I don't recommend another Pap test," she said. "Instead, I suggest that you have a biopsy. We'll take some tissue from your cervix and send it to the lab, and that will give us a much better idea of what we are dealing with."

Since I do not have a medical degree and her recommendation seemed wise, I had the biopsy that same morning. Many women reading this book know the uneasy feeling you have while waiting for the results of a biopsy. For those of you who have never personally experienced this, trust me when I tell you that worrying appears to be one of the most plausible options (and probably one of the most widely selected).

"When will my results be in?" I asked.

"It may take up to two weeks," the assistant replied.

I kept thinking that surely in this age of men on the moon, email, and instant mashed potatoes, they could find out about my health a little sooner. But I held my tongue and said I would be waiting to hear from them. Then I drove home, worrying just a little.

The medical procedure I had just experienced was not a big deal. "A little uncomfortable," I believe was how the doctor described it but definitely not a major procedure.

When I got home I was mildly sick to my stomach so I went up to the bedroom to lie down. Unfortunately, I was not tired, and after twenty minutes of staring at the ceiling fan, I decided maybe I could accomplish some work while lying in a horizontal position. I also realized that working would give me something else to worry—oops!—think about besides my health.

My laptop computer was close by, and I propped up my back and head and put the computer, case and all, on my stomach. As I unzipped the case, a greeting card fell out of the pocket. It was

a card I had purchased weeks before to put in my card stash—
a collection of cards waiting to be mailed at the appropriate
time to the appropriate person. I was astonished as I looked
at the card.

On the front was a cartoon picture of a skier with great big
eyes going off an obviously unexpected jump. The caption read,
"Be anxious for nothing . . ." Inside it read: "God is still in control!" In a way, I had sent myself a greeting card! Unless you
have a really bad memory, that doesn't happen too often.

I smiled and marveled at the goodness of God's provision.
I needed the reminder, and He knew it! Even though I knew
Betty's story and I'd seen her peace and lack of worry firsthand,
I needed to be reminded: *Choose not to worry, Kendra. Don't
live in your What Ifs.*

I am thankful for the reminder, and I am thankful that on
that day I was able to make the choice not to worry, even before
the biopsy results—showing no cancer—were in. I am also
thankful that God has given me an example like Betty. She is
a woman whose life circumstances were fertile ground for
worry, and yet with God's help she has chosen not to worry.
I've never heard her say, "If only Pete hadn't hit me. . . . If only
our two daughters had a decent father. . . . If only Pete hadn't
lied about being a Christian. . . ."

Through Betty's life and story, God reminds me not to
worry. His love letter, the Bible, is filled with reminders not to
worry. God encourages all of us, regardless of our situations,
to choose not to worry. Perhaps it is *your* next right choice.

✻   ✻   ✻

So do not fear, for I am with you; do not be dismayed, for I am your God.
I will strengthen you and help you; I will uphold you with my righteous right hand.

Isaiah 41:10

✻   ✻   ✻

CHOOSE TO
Reflect

Philippians 4:6 says, "Do not be anxious about anything, but in everything, by prayer and petition, with thanksgiving, present your requests to God." God does not just tell you what not to do ("Do not be anxious"). He also tells you what He wants you to do ("present your requests" to Him "by prayer and petition, with thanksgiving").

Lord, You know that today I've been worrying about _____. I'm giving that concern to You. Thank You for being willing to take my worries and anxieties. Thank You for caring for me. Amen.

STUDY QUESTIONS

Choose Not to Worry

1. Read Matthew 6:25–34. What does Matthew say about being anxious? Have you ever allowed worry to control your actions?

2. What things cause you to worry (health, finances, family, potential accidents, etc.)?

3. If "worry consumes priceless, irreplaceable energy," how have you seen that evident in your own life?

4. Why is it difficult to release control of our lives to God?

5. How might you apply Matthew's teaching "do not be anxious about tomorrow" to the concerns you have today?

6

CHOOSE TO BE CONTENT

But godliness with contentment is great gain.

1 TIMOTHY 6:6

Joan wandered down the hall to the small waiting room attached to the newborns' nursery. She felt remarkably perky, considering that she had given birth to a baby girl just hours before. The labor had been easy and delivery had been very quick. Baby Elizabeth's APGAR score (a test that measures the responses of a newborn) was a healthy eight, and the infant had nursed eagerly in the birthing room. After a while, nurses had taken Elizabeth to the nursery to clean her up. Joan's husband, Greg, had gone to the phone to notify relatives, and Joan had closed her eyes to rest.

Now, an hour or so later, Joan, refreshed and ready to spend more time with her little girl, wandered down to the nursery and entered the small waiting room attached to the babies' room.

The door was ajar, and as Joan relaxed in a rocker, waiting for a nurse to emerge, she heard bits and snatches of conversation—just isolated words and pieces of dialogue. "Mom sick?" "Rubella?" "Retarded . . ." "Head size . . ." "Handicapped . . ."

"I knew they were talking about Elizabeth, and my heart began to break into a million pieces," Joan told me years later as she related the facts of that day. "They never mentioned my name or Greg's or Elizabeth's, but I knew that the concerned conversation was about us. Moments later Greg joined me. As we both heard more sentence fragments, our concern grew. Finally a doctor came out of the nursery door and saw us sitting in the room adjacent to the nursery. He had no idea how long we had been sitting there."

He began to speak, but Joan interrupted him. "We have a problem, don't we?" Joan questioned. The doctor nodded his head.

*　　　*　　　*

A partnership with God is motherhood.
Mary Wood Allen

*　　　*　　　*

Joan had been teaching school while pregnant. In her sixth month, she contracted a virus—cytomegalovirus. This virus rarely causes serious disease in healthy people, but when an expectant mother becomes infected during pregnancy, the infant is at risk for congenital infection. The virus was probably carried to her classroom by one of her students, who may not even have appeared ill. Joan, however, contracted the virus and became very sick. She sensed at that time that things were not right with her pregnancy.

"I am not a worrier," Joan told Greg one day. "You know that. It's just that I can't seem to shake the feeling that something is wrong."

Greg had no particular answers to his wife's concerns. He always comforted and reassured her that God had everything under control.

Late one night Joan was lying awake in bed. As she lay there, she began to pray—to talk to God about all the things that were on her mind. As she scrolled through the day's events and the joys and challenges they had brought, she realized that her greatest concern was for her unborn baby. She was concerned the baby had been affected somehow by her illness.

"Lord, You know the concern of my heart. It is not a fear that something is wrong but rather a strong feeling. It's almost like a message from You, but I'm not sure. Is that what it is? Are You telling me something about our little baby? Was the baby hurt by my illness?" Joan honestly questioned the Lord, but how could she know the answer? "If my concern is warranted, God," she ventured, "please have the baby kick."

Although mother and child had been lying completely still for hours, at the precise moment of Joan's statement, the unborn child kicked with great force. It was such a hard kick that Joan could not ignore it or pretend it hadn't happened. But still she questioned whether it was God responding to her prayer or whether it was her own imagination.

Joan pondered the midnight conversation with the Lord for several days. She became more and more convinced the baby's kick had been no coincidence. She decided it must have been from God. Joan decided to mimic the fleeces of Gideon.

Gideon said to God, "If you will save Israel by my hand as you have promised—look, I will place a wool fleece on the threshing floor. If there is dew only on the fleece and all the ground is dry, then I will know that you will save Israel by my hand, as you said." And that is what happened. Gideon rose early the next day; he squeezed the fleece and wrung out the dew—a bowl full of water.

Then Gideon said to God, "Do not be angry with me. Let me

make just one more request. Allow me one more test with the fleece, but this time make the fleece dry and let the ground be covered with dew." That night God did so. Only the fleece was dry; all the ground was covered with dew. (Judges 6:36–40)

"God, if there is something wrong with this baby," Joan said, "do not allow him or her to kick any more until birth." And that is precisely what happened. The child did not kick again before birth.

*   *   *

As a mother, my job is to take care of the possible and trust God with the impossible.
Ruth Bell Graham

*   *   *

Now, sitting in the nursery of the hospital, Joan looked up at the physician and asked, "We have a problem, don't we?" already knowing the answer in her heart.

"We have a very serious problem," he answered. "Your little girl is severely mentally retarded."

Little Elizabeth was just hours old. Her parents, who should have been experiencing great joy at her birth, were instead experiencing grief. She was alive, but the dream they had for her life died along with the doctor's words. He was saying that Elizabeth would never go to kindergarten, learn to tie her shoes, roller skate, stay up all night at slumber parties, chatter on the telephone, graduate from high school, attend college, marry, or have babies of her own. They really didn't understand how much they had lost that day. It was vague. Yet Joan and Greg knew their dream of raising a little girl and experiencing all the typical little girl joys and sorrows was dead. They began to grieve their loss, the loss of a dream and a vision for Elizabeth.

According to modern psychology, there are five stages of

grief. The first one is denial. Joan and Greg, however, did not experience denial, at least not to the degree that it is typically expressed.

Joan's acceptance of the situation was considered by some to be a form of denial in itself. Some said she must not have realized the severity of the circumstances since she seemed to accept them so readily. There was, however, another possibility, another way to explain the attitude that Joan and Greg shared.

Although denial is typically the first stage of grief, even psychologists admit that the intensity and severity of this stage can be controlled to some degree. The key is the presentation of the tragedy—its timing and the presenter himself.

"This anxious denial following the presentation of a diagnosis is more typical of the patient who is informed prematurely or abruptly by someone who does not know the patient well, or does it quickly 'to get it over with' without taking the patient's readiness into consideration."[7]

No one could possibly know Joan better or love her more than God. He was the One who had gently broken the news to her in the stillness of the night. And God's timing is always perfect. Because God revealed what was about to happen, her stage of denial was shortened and perhaps had even been completed by the time the doctor made his announcement on the day of Elizabeth's birth. Maybe denial had been eliminated altogether.

In a normal grief process, denial is followed by anger. In a situation like this, one can imagine a whole list of people who could have been recipients of Joan's anger. She could have chosen to be angry with her physician. Perhaps he had made an error in treatment that had led to this difficulty. If only he had done his job well.

She could have been mad at the children from whom she had contracted the virus. If only they had stayed home from school. She could have chosen to be angry with the parents of those children. If only they had known their kids were contagious. She could have been angry with God. If only He had protected her. If only He had not allowed this to happen.

But Joan chose not to be angry with her physician, the hospital, the children she had taught, their parents, or with God. Perhaps even more importantly, she chose to be content, not to be jealous of others whose circumstances were more fortunate—whose children were normal.

*   *   *

Anger is cruel and fury overwhelming,
but who can stand before jealousy?
Proverbs 27:4

*   *   *

Jealousy is a very powerful and a very negative emotion that wars against our ability to accept all that happens to us as coming from the hands of a good God. Anger and fury in all their magnitude are still outdone by jealousy. Jealousy can ruin a friendship, a family, and the individual who harbors it. It is destructive both to the one who carries it and to the one who is its recipient.

Can you see how Joan might have been tempted to let jealousy reign in her life? Elizabeth would never do the things other little girls do. That certainly was not fair. Joan might have thought about giving up teaching. Perhaps if she simply refused to help any other child develop, Elizabeth's handicap would not appear so great. Why should Joan be interested in teaching concepts and ideas to other parents' perfectly healthy kids when Elizabeth would be able to learn very little herself? Let their mothers teach them! Why, a child just getting ready to go to school had already learned things that Elizabeth would never learn!

*　　*　　*

For I have learned to be content

whatever the circumstances.

Philippians 4:11

*　　*　　*

"God calls me to be content—not complacent but content. Comparing Elizabeth with other children is pointless. That's where jealousy begins," Joan said. "That is like comparing your home with another's or the achievements of your children with the achievements of other people's children. The comparison can lead to arrogance (if you choose to compare to a lesser home or achiever) or to jealousy. After all, you can always find a more palatial dwelling or a more motivated or decorated achiever."

Joan was seeking God's wisdom. "I want to be content with what God has allowed to happen," she said. "It matters so much more what I do in the circumstances than what the circumstances are."

Joan chose contentment versus comparison. She was proactive, not reactive, in response to her circumstances. When we are tempted to react in jealousy, we need to remind ourselves to quit comparing, to be accepting, and to learn contentment. Try to begin to see the many reasons you have for contentment. Comparison is a game with no winners.

Joan found other responses that helped her choose to accept her circumstances. She chose to exercise her talents rather than her torments. She had been trained as a teacher, and she was a very good one. When I first met her, she was teaching kindergarten. Her enthusiasm for children and for learning was obvious and contagious. I remember being in her kindergarten classroom during a lesson on the importance of hand washing to prevent the spread of germs. Joan took a red washable marker and colored a portion of the palm of her hand with it.

"This marker color is just like germs. I need to wash my hands before I eat to wash away the germs," she explained. "Look what happens when I don't."

She shook hands with the children in her class, and one by one their hands turned red as the marker rubbed off on their palms.

"The marker stain is like the germs that are on our hands. Real germs are invisible. You can't see them," Joan explained to her eager students. "And they pass from one person to another very easily. They move just as easily as this marker stain moved from my hand to yours. We need to wash before we eat so that the germs don't get on our food."

The kids understood. They didn't want to be the ones who passed germs to other children.

The lesson was a hit, and as soon as they were allowed, each kindergartener washed off the marker stain with great relish. They didn't want to spread any germs or marker stains!

How ironic, I thought. Little children just like these probably gave cytomegalovirus to Joan. Lovable kids like these gave her the virus that resulted in Elizabeth's retardation. While Joan could have been angry or jealous or discontent, she was not. She just went on doing a great job of teaching this group of young children—teaching them concepts, ideas, and facts that her daughter would never learn, never be able to grasp.

Who would have blamed Joan if she had chosen to lock away her teaching talents and never use them again? Did anyone expect her to invest herself in healthy kids when she had to care for Elizabeth? Who would have misunderstood if she had chosen to be bitter and to torment herself and others with her pain? Talents or torments: For Joan the choice was clear. Her choice not to be jealous of others and to accept her situation allowed her to exercise her talents in teaching.

Joan did not ask, "Why?" "Why?" questions have no answers. "Why did I get sick when I was pregnant?" "Why was my baby affected by the virus?" "Why is Elizabeth retarded?"

Joan chose to ask "What?" questions. "What can I learn from this situation?" "What can I teach others?" "What?" questions move us further along in accepting our circumstances.

Joan learned almost immediately the importance of graciously accepting any display of kindness or concern with respect to Elizabeth.

"People responded to Elizabeth in different ways, and they still do," Joan explained. "There are some who greet her cheerfully: 'Oh, hi, Elizabeth. How are you doing?' Then, because of her cerebral palsy, they have to wait for eight to ten seconds for her to respond to them with a smile or a laugh. There are other folks who act as though Elizabeth is invisible. They ask about her in her presence but never address her personally. And, of course, there are people who avoid any contact or connection with Elizabeth or with me when we are together."

God showed Joan very early how important it was to encourage all those reaching out to her. It is not easy to know what to say to a mother of a handicapped child. Joan decided that she would appreciate any attempt at encouragement or consolation even if it was an awkward attempt. She knew people were trying to minister to her and to Elizabeth in their own, sometimes fumbling ways.

"It is pointless to think less of someone who is uncomfortable," Joan explained. "He or she is responding to the degree of his or her ability to respond. I am just grateful for any acknowledgment of our situation. I've decided to accept any comfort, even if it is misguided. When people say something that could be interpreted as insensitive, I silently say, 'They don't mean this maliciously. They just want to minister to me. Okay, they didn't do it just right, but I'm going to take it for what it is—a hand extended in friendship.'"

Joan didn't learn this gracious response on her own. She learned it from God. And she's taught me, and others who know her, a great deal about the gracious acceptance of the words of others.

Joan has also taught me that there are no perfect words to speak to someone in crisis or who has had something devastating happen in his or her life. So instead of waiting for perfect words, just say *something* to a hurting person. Do the best you can, and leave the rest to God. This doesn't mean that I charge into a tragedy just to show up. It does mean that as friends experience difficult situations, I show them some expression of my caring. The friend who has lost a loved one, or is feeling the pangs of a rebellious child, or is experiencing grief in any form needs to know that I know she hurts and that I care. Joan's example has encouraged me to speak in love.

"When little children see Elizabeth bobbing in her wheelchair, they wonder what is wrong with her. I smile at them and sometimes even say, 'Elizabeth is retarded. She can see the bright colors in your shirts, and she likes them.' These kids are curious, but they are not cruel," Joan explains. "I try to appreciate their attention and encourage it. Elizabeth does."

Joan also learned that even Elizabeth could have a ministry to others. When Elizabeth was seven months old, Joan started a physical therapy program called patterning. Joan's and Greg's home was located within blocks of the Christian school where Joan had taught. She organized a schedule, asked for volunteers, and the patterning began. Five times a day, for thirty minutes each time, three people provided physical stimulus to Elizabeth. They also laid hands on her and prayed for her. It was a positive experience for everyone involved.

Elizabeth's cheerful countenance and good nature were a blessing to everyone who volunteered. Her appreciative attitude reminded those around her to count their blessings. "The men and women who came to help me had a real ministry to Elizabeth," Joan said. "I was able to minister to them, and amazingly Elizabeth ministered to them too. It was an incredible time."

The patterning therapy continued until Elizabeth was two. Then the school relocated, and other factors let Joan know it was time to do something different. What had Joan learned? She had learned that everyone can have a ministry. It is not limited by mental ability.

*   *   *

I praise you because

I am fearfully and wonderfully made.

Psalm 139:14

*   *   *

With the birth of Elizabeth, Joan also learned in a firsthand way about the sanctity of human life. And how does Joan feel about pro-life versus pro-choice?

"I was quizzing a candidate for state representative and I asked him his stance on pro-choice and pro-life. 'Oh,' he replied, 'I'm pro-life,' but then he started waffling, 'unless of course the unborn child is retarded. Then the woman should have the right to terminate the pregnancy.'"

He paused, and Joan stepped right in. "*How* interesting. I have a severely mentally retarded child. Her name is Elizabeth, and I am very grateful that her life was not terminated."

At that point the air was so thick you could cut it with a knife. Joan is very gracious to those who are even slightly uncomfortable with Elizabeth, but she is not tolerant of politicians—policy makers—who are not willing to support the sanctity of all human life. Such candidates will never get Joan's support.

When Joan declares that all life is precious, she knows that it is. She comes from a different vantage point than the average citizen or parent. She's had firsthand experience. God has taught her just how precious life is, and now she teaches others.

Joan's grief was proactive. She chose contentment over comparison, talents over torture, and acceptance over jealousy. She asked the question, "What can I learn from this situation that I can in turn teach others?" She saw the importance of appreciating gestures of kindness and teaching others to respond to hurting people in kindness and in love. She learned to acknowledge the potential ministry of people in all stations of life and to teach others this truth. She also grasped, beyond the average person's ability, the truth of the sanctity of human life.

*   *   *

A child is a gift whose worth
cannot be measured except by the heart.
Theresa Ann Hunt

*   *   *

And how did Joan handle the last stages of grief? They are typically viewed as bargaining, depression, and ultimately acceptance.

"I don't believe in the God/rock theory," Joan told me one day. "That's where God sits up in heaven and arbitrarily throws rocks at people. That theory shows God to be capricious and indiscriminate, like He has no plan for a life."

If you believe in the sovereign power of God, there is no need to bargain. You understand that He has a plan for each life.

And depression? "The day Elizabeth would have gone to school was 'one of those moments' that you have as the mother of a retarded child," Joan explained. "On the first day of kindergarten, Elizabeth, of course, did not attend school. I cried throughout the day as once again the reality of her handicap reared its ugly head. My Elizabeth would never go to 'real school.'"

Instead, Elizabeth attended a class for the profoundly mentally retarded. The ratio of teacher-aide/social worker to student is almost one-on-one, and Elizabeth received excellent instruction.

Elizabeth cannot walk. An army crawl takes her from room to room at home. Away from home she moves only as someone else pushes her wheelchair. She has a sum total of three words in her vocabulary.

"Elizabeth can't say 'momma' or 'mommy.' Those words take fine motor skills she cannot develop," Joan said. Elizabeth can sign for hungry and thirsty and will occasionally signal when she has to go to the bathroom.

*   *   *

A mother understands what a child does not say.

Jewish proverb

*   *   *

Does all of this depress Joan? She has her moments, but if depression is defined as a condition that impairs normal functioning, then the answer is no. Elizabeth is mentally retarded, and Joan has accepted the fact.

Joan is often asked, "How do you handle a profoundly mentally retarded child?" She tells those who ask, "You help her to be the best she can be, and you try never to get stuck in neutral. I know that God wants me to move forward in life and to grow. I want to grow spiritually and professionally in all areas. He does not want me to blame Elizabeth or use her handicap as an excuse for complacency, anger, or jealousy."

There are no "if onlys" or "what ifs" for Joan and her family. Would life have been different without Elizabeth? Of course. It might have been much easier. But Joan tells the other side of it. "I might have been arrogant and self-serving without Elizabeth," she says. "Being the parent of a profoundly mentally retarded child is humbling—very humbling," Joan admits. Because she gave birth to Elizabeth, a wonderful young lady who is profoundly mentally retarded, Joan had choices to make, and she chose not to be jealous of those who have it easier because they do not have a disabled child. She chose to be content. Because of her choices and attitude, she has made a significant investment in the lives of not only her own children but also those of countless others. Being content was her next right choice.

CHOOSE TO
Reflect

Our contentment does not have to be based on our circumstances. In fact, it is difficult to be content if we are allowing our circumstances to be in control. Contentment is not automatic. It is learned: "For I have learned to be content whatever the circumstances" (Philippians 4:11). Learning to be content is a choice, an empowering choice.

STUDY QUESTIONS

Choose to Be Content

1. Read Philippians 4:10-13. What were Paul's "highs" and what were his "lows"? What is Paul's secret to contentment?
2. What is the difference between being content and being complacent?
3. Jealousy is powerful. Have you ever experienced its negative effect?
4. The question *Why?* may have no answer. Is there something in your life that might prompt the question *What?*
5. The comments of others can negatively affect our feelings of contentment. Have you ever received misguided, unintentionally negative words from a friend? Have you ever spoken such words? How could you choose better words next time?
6. What ministry has God given you?

7

CHOOSE
TO RESPOND

You have two options. . . . You can choose
to respond—which is positive.
Or you can choose to react—which is negative.

Zig Ziglar, *Top Performance*

R-r-r-r-r-ing! The resounding phone startled Sonnie and Bob awake. Although the clock said a little after 5:00 a.m., it felt like the middle of the night. R-r-r-r-r-ing! This time the summons caused Bob to jump out of bed and go to the phone. R-r-r-r . . . The third ring was cut short as he lifted the handset.

"Hello," Bob said and then paused. "Yes, we have a son named Eric. Yes, he was wearing Reebok shoes. Yes, he was driving a blue Citation. An accident? Where? How is Eric?"

Questions flooded Sonnie's mind, too, as she was suddenly wide awake and frightened. The answers to those questions would have to wait for an hour or so. Bob hung up the phone, told Sonnie the few details he had learned, and they dressed as rapidly as they could. As they raced to the hospital, the day was dawning and the nightmare was beginning.

* * *

**Therefore, prepare your minds for action;
be self-controlled; set your hope fully on the grace
to be given you when Jesus Christ is revealed.**
1 Peter 1:13

* * *

Isn't it strange how quickly life can change? One day can be so calm, peaceful, and predictable, and the next can be filled with drama, anxiety, and trauma.

Friday had been one of those calm, peaceful, predictable days. Sonnie had gone to work at her flower shop. Bob was at work on the farm. Their son, Eric, home from college for the summer, had put in a full day at his summer job at the high school.

Eric had just finished his freshman year in college at a small school in Tennessee. He had been offered, and had accepted, a full baseball scholarship to Benedictine College in Chicago and was to begin in the fall. It was an exciting time for him, filled with great expectations.

His summer job had been going well. He worked with nice people, and his paycheck was a good addition to his college fund. On Friday, after he deposited his check and did some errands, he went to his mom's shop to visit for a minute.

"I deposited my paycheck after work," Eric reported. "And then I mowed Grandma's lawn. Now I'm going to head home and get cleaned up. Then I'm going down to the junior college for my class."

"What time is your class?" his mom asked.

"Not until 7:00 p.m., so I have plenty of time," Eric replied.

"Well, have a good time," Sonnie said. "We'll mow our lawn tomorrow. Bye, honey!"

"Bye, Mom," Eric shouted over his shoulder as he went out the door.

This would be their last conversation for many months.

*　　　*　　　*

Fear not, for I have redeemed you;

I have summoned you by name; you are mine.

When you pass through the waters,

I will be with you; and when you pass through

the rivers, they will not sweep over you.

Isaiah 43:1–2

*　　　*　　　*

Sonnie and Bob rushed into the hospital and were greeted by the state police and by medical professionals. The strangers tried to explain what had happened at the accident site. It had been a one-car accident with no witnesses, so they pieced the evidence together to the best of their ability.

"It doesn't appear that your son was driving too fast," the officer explained. "Since there were no other cars involved, we feel certain that he merely fell asleep at the wheel and lost control."

"How is he?" Sonnie asked. "Where is he?"

Now it was the physician's turn to reply.

"Eric has suffered a severe closed-wound trauma to his head," the emergency room doctor explained. "We do not expect him to survive more than twenty-four hours. His condition is very tenuous. The next few hours are critical."

Sonnie and Bob were in shock. The news was almost overwhelming. How could something like this have happened to Eric? He was so strong and alert—a healthy young man anticipating such an exciting future. What were his parents supposed to do now, in light of this terrible, terrible news?

What, indeed, were they to do? They had choices to make. Immediately they began to pray for guidance. They knew that even though their private world seemed to be spinning out of control, God was still in control.

*　　　*　　　*

Trust in the Lord with all your heart

and lean not on your own understanding;

in all your ways acknowledge him,

and he will make your paths straight.

Proverbs 3:5–6

*　　　*　　　*

That day and night were long for Eric's family. His brothers, who lived nearby, joined in the vigil as Eric struggled through the next twenty-four hours. Their emotions were ragged as the family members dealt with the fact that Eric might not live.

That kind of harsh reality can evoke many reactions and responses. The most typical reaction is shock and disbelief. *Maybe that wasn't our Eric in the accident. Maybe this is just a bad dream and I'll wake up soon.*

We can react with anger and frustration and list our "if onlys." *If only Eric had gone to bed earlier the night before, he wouldn't have been tired enough to fall asleep at the wheel. If only he had taken the truck instead of that little car. If only he hadn't enrolled in summer school.*

We can choose to react with a knee-jerk type of reflex: *Something happened that I don't like and BAM!! I'm striking back.* Or we can respond. A response is a thinking reply, a reply governed by self-control.

After the initial shock, pain, and disbelief, Sonnie and her family chose to respond rather than to react. During the next twenty-four-hour period, they emotionally released Eric to God.

"We prayed that God's will would be done in Eric's life," Sonnie explained. "Only God knew if it was better for Eric to live or die."

The family chose to respond to the life-and-death situation by asking God to take charge. They chose a thinking reply to the trauma, not a reaction. Their choice to respond, although extremely difficult, was made easier by something that had happened earlier in the year. In February, Eric had given his testimony at their home church and had been baptized.

"I knew I wanted to do it," he told his mom after the church service. "What would I say to Jesus if He came back today and looked me in the face and said, 'I died on the cross so you could have eternal life. Why haven't you had the courage to stand up and accept My gift?'"

That evening had been such a glorious blessing for Sonnie and all of Eric's family. He unashamedly declared his love for Jesus. This witness made the events that were to occur months later fall into perspective. True, Eric was hanging between life and death, but his death would merely mean a passing from this life to a better one with Jesus.

With that assurance, Eric's family chose to respond to the tragic events by asking God to have His way.

*   *   *

Be joyful in hope,
patient in affliction, faithful in prayer.
Romans 12:12

*   *   *

Eric lived through those twenty-four hours. Amazingly, his vital signs began to stabilize, and before long his respiration and heart rate were almost normal. He was, however, in a coma. He lay in his hospital bed, unable to speak, move, or respond in any way. His body was alive, but his brain, the clearinghouse of the central nervous system, was damaged greatly.

Was this God's will? Sonnie had really believed that initially there were only two options: Eric would die and be with Jesus, or Eric would regain his health. She hadn't considered the possibility that he would be comatose, at least not for so many days.

The days turned into weeks and the weeks turned into months. Eric did not respond in any manner. Occasionally his body would react with a reflexive action, but months passed with no thinking response.

How does a mother respond in this situation? Daily, Sonnie had to choose response versus reaction, and each day it became more difficult.

"After Eric had been in a coma for six months," Sonnie said, "I realized that my hope was almost spent. It was so difficult not to react in anger or frustration."

And then one day Eric's main physician made a suggestion. "I think Eric has fluid around his brain keeping him from responding," said the doctor. "It is possible that if we do surgery and install a shunt into his skull to drain the fluid, we might see improvement. There are, however, two things you must consider. Number one, this surgery may not help Eric at all, and number two, the surgery is extremely dangerous and could end Eric's life."

It was a difficult decision. Eric's parents pondered it with little peace. Their reaction was to avoid the risk. After all, the two considerations the doctor gave them were both so negative it was hard to imagine any possible success from the endeavor.

"No, we're not going to give permission for the shunt surgery," they told their older children. "It's just too risky."

"But what have we got to lose?" asked their eldest son. "Eric has not responded to anyone or anything since the accident six months ago. This surgery might give him a chance. How can we choose not to give permission?"

That question started Sonnie thinking. Her oldest son was right. The surgery was not a risk. It was an opportunity. The initial decision not to schedule the shunt surgery had been a reaction, a reflex, and not a thinking reply or response. Now they looked at the options and chose to schedule the surgery.

Eric came through the shunt surgery well. There was, however, no dramatic change. On his rounds each day, Eric's doctor would enter the room and in his booming voice ask, "Well, how's my boy Eric doing today?"

Then Sonnie would answer, "Oh, he's just doing great!"

"Here, Eric," the doctor would bark. "Here's my hand. Squeeze my hand, Eric."

Day after day after day there would be no response, and the doctor would continue to his next patient. But one day things were different.

"Here, Eric. Here's my hand. Squeeze my hand, Eric," the doctor commanded.

*   *   *

A man's wisdom gives him patience.

Proverbs 19:11

*   *   *

And Eric did! The look on the doctor's face said it all.

"Well, well, well," he began. "This is quite a Christmas gift, Mom and Dad. Eric is beginning to respond."

After months in an impenetrable coma, Eric responded with a squeeze of his doctor's hand. The risky surgery had indeed made a difference. Eric's progress was painfully slow. Nothing changed overnight or dramatically. In tiny, tiny increments he continued to improve. At the one-year anniversary of his near fatal accident, he still was unable to speak, although he

103

was regaining some ability to move. Time marched on, and Eric worked very hard to move forward in his therapy.

At times Sonnie had a terrific struggle with patience. Hadn't she been patient enough? It had been six months, eight months, twelve months, and now sixteen months, and still Eric had not spoken one word. It was difficult to keep choosing to respond to Eric and to his situation.

On Thanksgiving weekend, nearly eighteen months after the accident, Eric was allowed to come home for an overnight stay. His motor skills had improved to the point that he could sit up in his wheelchair. He was aware of his surroundings, recognized his family, and obviously enjoyed being with them. He was, however, on a feeding tube and still could not speak a word.

Sonnie was nervous, but the overnight visit went well. The next afternoon, Eric's father packed up his things and took him back to the hospital. It was a long drive, so he planned to spend the night and drive back home the next day. Several hours after he and Eric had left, Sonnie received a phone call from them. The trip had been uneventful. They had arrived back at the hospital, and Eric was settling in.

"Oh, and I have a little surprise for you," said Eric's father, Bob. "Eric, Mom is on the phone. Here, listen to Mom say hi."

"Hi, Eric!" Sonnie said cheerfully. "It's Mom. It was great to have you home for Thanksgiving. I love you."

"M-m-a-m," Eric said into the receiver.

Eric *said*? Yes, he was speaking. It was not easy to understand, but he was saying something. He was saying "Mom."

Eric was responding to therapy. Parts of his brain were slowly healing.

Eric's recovery continued to provide both him and his mother with opportunities to respond. Eric's response was what every doctor, nurse, and therapist was striving for. Sonnie's responses were choices she had to make daily. Each day she had the option to react or to respond. Her goal was to respond, to give a thinking reply to Eric and to those around him.

Early in the rehabilitation process, one of Eric's physicians had told Sonnie that the old Eric was gone. Sonnie's initial reaction to that statement was to refuse to believe it.

"Eric will get better," she thought. "My old Eric will be back."

Sonnie didn't want to entertain the thought that the Eric she had known and loved for nineteen years was gone forever. That thought was too painful.

Slowly, however, she realized that perhaps the physician had been correct. Sonnie's denial did nothing to change the situation. Perhaps it was even doing harm.

"One day I realized that my old Eric was truly gone, and that the doctor was right when he said he'd never return," Sonnie admitted. "It was then I chose to let go of the old Eric, so that there was room for the new one. I chose to get to know and love my new son."

Sonnie went from reaction to response. She allowed the new Eric to become her son. "I like the new Eric," Sonnie told me. "He has got to be one of the most pleasant and thankful people I have ever known. He's so grateful, even for little things like singing in church or eating dinner. He thanks his dad and me all the time."

I've gotten to know the new Eric, and I like him too. Anyone would! He is a hard worker, with God's direction, determination, and perseverance. After eleven years he has regained more and more physical ability. It is still extremely difficult for Eric to communicate verbally, although it is not impossible for him to speak and be understood.

Eric can now walk without a walker or crutches, although his right side is partially paralyzed. He has learned to eat with his left hand, and his smile, though perhaps a little crooked, is very engaging. His mother is right: Eric is pleasant and thankful.

One evening, Sonnie, Eric, and I were enjoying a pizza together when we heard his dad's truck pull up the lane. "I'll bet that's Dad," Sonnie said to Eric. "Maybe he is taking a break from picking corn."

"Da–aaad," Eric repeated with great joy and excitement. "Daaad."

Eric rose slightly from his seat to see if it was his father coming in. Eric's response was pure, unashamed joy. He could hardly wait to see his dad.

Sonnie's response was delight. She loved her new Eric and enjoyed sharing in his excitement that Dad was home.

*　　*　　*

O Lord, you have searched me and you know me.

You know when I sit and when I rise;

you perceive my thoughts from afar.

Psalm 139:1–2

*　　*　　*

We all have many opportunities each day to choose either to react or to respond. Usually events aren't as monumental or as long-playing as Sonnie's and Eric's. We react or respond to our families, our coworkers, the people we meet in the grocery store. Responding means controlling the tongue.

*　　*　　*

He who guards his lips guards his life.

Proverbs 13:3

*　　*　　*

Years ago I headed up a team of workers putting together a convention. There were many details that were important to the success of the convention. In order to assure that we would attend to those details efficiently and effectively, I developed an easy plan. At our team meetings I would ask for volunteers to accept the various responsibilities. As people volunteered, I would note their names on my list at the same time I saw them adding the task to their lists. That, I thought, would assure that every base was covered and no detail would be forgotten.

The week of the convention finally arrived, and things were going smoothly. One particular detail that a team member had written on her list was the purchase of poster board for one of our speakers. Judy had volunteered for that task and about forty-five minutes before this particular speaker was to appear, I approached Judy to ask where she had put the poster board.

"You never told me to buy poster board," she said defensively.

I knew for a fact that I had indeed asked her to buy poster board. I had made a note of it on my list when I saw her put it on her list. I had to fight the overwhelming urge to react. I could have said, "I *know* you volunteered to get poster board. There is no doubt in my mind. You *just forgot,* didn't you?"

I could have said that. It would not have been very kind or considerate. It would not have been a thinking reply. And it would not have gotten me poster board. Instead, through the grace of God, I said to myself, "Kendra, what is your goal?" That question, by the way, is an excellent way to increase your chances of responding rather than reacting.

What was my goal? That's right! It was to get poster board. So, instead of ranting and raving and proving I was right and she was wrong, I took a deep breath and said, "Whew! We need poster board. Do you think you can find any?"

"Well," she said, "I could probably take the rental car and run down the block to the discount store."

"Great idea," I replied, and off she went.

The poster board arrived in plenty of time. The speaker was a happy camper, and so was my coworker. Thank goodness I remembered to ask myself, "What is my goal?" That was a good choice, and it sent me in the direction of a positive attitude.

Unfortunately I don't always make that good choice. Sometimes I choose to react. On one particular evening in early February, I witnessed a distressing basketball game. Our eldest son, who was sixteen at the time, played on a team that was young and inexperienced. That night they were matched with a more accomplished team. The result was a frustrating, one-sided game. Way beyond the impact of the score, however, was the fact that our young players were bombarded with nasty comments and unkind remarks throughout the game. It was a negative experience.

When the game finally ended, our son grabbed his coat, trousers, and gym bag and told his coach he was riding home with us. He was exhausted from spending the evening in this demoralizing situation. As our family walked outside, the boys and my husband, John, were a few feet ahead of me. The cold air hit my face, and I suddenly realized that Matthew had not put his coat on yet.

"Matthew, put your coat on," I told him.

This eldest child who usually responded in an immediate manner did nothing. His sweaty, slumping shoulders remained uncovered.

"Matthew, it's cold outside. Please put your coat on," I repeated.

When there was still no response, I prepared to give the order a final time with more conviction. As I began to speak, my second son, Aaron, slipped back a few steps to walk with me.

He reached over, touched my arm, and said, "Mom, you've got to know when to hold 'em and know when to fold 'em."

Wow! Wisdom out of the mouths of babes (teens actually). Aaron was 100 percent correct. I was reacting. I wasn't giving a thinking response. If I had been thinking, I would have realized that at that moment, Matthew did not need my advice about dressing for conditions. Instead he needed the assurance of my unconditional love.

What was my goal? Aaron reminded me to ask that question. Sometimes it takes a little reminder from a loved one to help us choose to respond rather than to react.

* * *

Not only to say the right thing in the right place,

but far more difficult, to leave unsaid

the wrong thing at the tempting moment.

Benjamin Franklin

* * *

Sonnie chose to respond to the initial shock of Eric's accident rather than to react in anger. Sonnie and her family found peace through their faith in God. Sonnie needed the reminder of her older children to help her respond to the decision about Eric's shunt surgery. Her reaction was "no." Her response—her thinking reply—was "yes." And finally, Sonnie chose to respond to the new Eric by letting go of the old Eric and making room for her "new" son.

Sonnie responded. She chose faith-filled, thinking replies. She could have chosen to react to Eric's accident and to his long and continual recovery period. Even today she could choose to react to his limited abilities, or she could choose to respond. Sonnie made the next right choice to respond—no "if onlys" or "what ifs." She continues to make that choice daily to respond to circumstances beyond her control with love, joy, and enthusiasm. And Eric responds to her.

"Every day I have a choice to spend the day indulging in self-pity or allowing the Lord to have victory as He refines me for His kingdom," Sonnie explained. "And I am here to tell you that God is able. When our hearts are broken by tragedy, Jesus holds every piece of our broken heart and if we allow Him, He will put each piece back together with His everlasting glue."

CHOOSE TO
Reflect

Scripture says, "Therefore, prepare your minds for action; be self-controlled; set your hope fully on the grace to be given when Jesus Christ is revealed" (1 Peter 1:13). *God's Word encourages us to be prepared and self-controlled. When we respond rather than react, chances are we are both prepared and self-controlled.*

STUDY QUESTIONS

Choose to Respond

1. What advice does Ephesians 4:25–32 give us for responding to challenging situations?

2. What is the primary difference between reacting and responding?

3. Can you identify a time when you chose to react? A time when you chose to respond? Which outcome was more positive?

4. Have you ever asked, "What is my goal?" How might that question be helpful?

5. Do you believe these words of Sonnie's: "When our hearts are broken by tragedy, Jesus holds every piece of our broken hearts. If we allow Him, He will put each piece back together with His everlasting glue"?

8

CHOOSE GENEROSITY

Let me live my life so that those to whom love is
a stranger will find in me a generous friend.

ROBERT BENSON

The conference was scheduled for a week in January. It
would be an understatement to say I was excited about getting away with good friends for a week of relaxing and growing in the Lord. About twenty-five women—all speakers and
writers—were gathering in Texas, and I was included in the
count.

Each day of the retreat began with a time of devotions. Several women had volunteered to take a turn leading, and I was
assigned day two.

The first day of devotions was very inspiring. Besides a short
message, the leader had copied a liturgy we all repeated. I don't
attend a liturgical church, so reading responsively wasn't a natural part of worship for me. Nevertheless one phrase of the

liturgy caught my attention: "Let me live my life so that those to whom love is a stranger will find in me a generous friend."

The next morning I was in charge. When I went to the meeting room to organize my thoughts, the devotional leader from the day before gave me a handout containing the same liturgy. "I want you to read this again today." As I nodded and accepted the printed piece, my thoughts went something like this: "Okay, I guess I can do this. It wasn't part of my plan, but that's no problem."

That day the same phrase seemed to shout at me: "Let me live my life so that those to whom love is a stranger will find in me a generous friend."

By the third morning of devotions I couldn't repeat that sentence without crying.

A "generous friend"—now that was something I wanted, I longed for—but truthfully I couldn't even define it. What did a generous friend look like? On that third morning my prayer became, "Please, Lord, show me what it looks like to be a generous friend." I did not have to wait long before my prayer was answered.

*   *   *

Ask and it will be given to you; seek and you will find;

knock and the door will be opened to you.

Matthew 7:7

*   *   *

The very next morning before devotions I was seated at the breakfast table with several others. "Kendra, what is wrong with you this morning?" one friend asked with a twinkle in her eye. "You're so quiet!"

She was right. I *was* being quiet. It was also completely legitimate to assume there was something wrong with that picture. I am a cheerful, talkative person AND a morning person. The combination can be lethal but not on that particular morning.

"Oh, sorry. My mind was somewhere else. In about one hour, my youngest son, Jonathan, is taking the dental aptitude test for the third time. He needs to score at least one point higher in order to be admitted to dental school. I'm busy thinking about him and praying for him."

My explanation was sufficient for the majority of those seated at the table, and they left the dining room. The women on my right and left, however, remained. "Let's pray together for your son. Let's pray right now." I couldn't have thought of a better idea.

The three of us joined hands in prayer. "Lord, please help Jonathan have clarity of thought. Help him recall the things he has learned." "Be with Kendra's dear son and help him feel Your peace as he takes this test." The prayers of my sweet friends continued for several minutes, but to be completely honest, after the first thirty seconds, I was no longer focused on the prayer concern.

You might wonder how that could be the case. After all it was *my* son who was the object of our prayers. It was his challenging day we were lifting to the Lord. How could Jonathan's own mother be distracted? And why? In order to answer those two questions, I need to provide you with essential background information.

*   *   *

There are some tragedies that are too big for a heart to hold, and they defy any description that makes sense.

Carol Kent

*   *   *

Seated to my right was my friend Carol Kent. It is quite possible you have heard of Carol or actually heard her, as she is a sought-after Christian speaker. Carol is also a mother, the mother of one son, J. P. I had never met J. P. just as she had never met my son, but I knew a great deal about his life. I gained the majority of my information from reading a poignant book written by Carol. *When I Lay My Isaac Down* is the account of the circumstances that occurred as her son's life took a tragic turn.

J. P. was a high achiever, a high school athlete, the president of the National Honor Society. He was a leader in his church youth group and a mentor to other students. From all accounts, this young man was a child any and every mother would be proud to call her own. After high school J. P. was granted an appointment to the Naval Academy in Annapolis, an honor limited to a very few. Those appointed are students who are at the top, mentally and physically, and who possess high character. The opportunity to attend the Academy and serve his country as a naval officer was fulfilling one of J. P.'s dreams for the future.

After graduation from Annapolis, J. P. was stationed in Florida. It was at this assignment that he met the woman who was to become his bride. April had been married before and was divorced. She had two beautiful daughters from her first marriage, and those little girls immediately found a place in J. P.'s heart. It seemed as though things could not be any better—a lovely wife, two wonderful stepdaughters, and, of course, a mother back home (my friend, Carol) who loved them all dearly.

But the story did not have a fairy-tale ending. The biological father of the little girls was still on the scene. There were multiple allegations of abuse, and it appeared that he was going to be given unsupervised visits with his daughters. Both J. P. and April had ominous feelings about that possibility and feared for the girls' safety. Unfortunately, J. P. began to unravel mentally, emotionally, and spiritually, and his fear resulted in an irrational, destructive action.

The *Orlando Sentinel* reported the sobering incident in this way:

BLEMISH FOR NAVY OFFICER—
MURDER CHARGE IN ORLANDO SHOOTING

Jason Kent [J. P.] crewed on the U.S. Naval Academy's offshore sailing team. His love for water was supposed to take him this week to the Pacific Ocean and his first duty as an officer aboard a ship anchored in Honolulu. But the young lieutenant might never again go to sea. He spends his days in the Orange County Jail awaiting trial on a first-degree murder charge.

An officer and a gentleman, Kent won't say a word about the burst of gunfire that killed his wife's ex-husband.[8]

J. P. was arrested, tried, and convicted of the crime of murder. Life would never be the same—not for J. P. or his wife or stepdaughters, not for Carol or anyone else who loved him.

Those are the facts you must know before I continue to tell you about my thoughts as my two dear friends and I prayed for my son's dental aptitude test that early morning in January. "Lord, please help Jonathan have clarity of thought. Help him recall the things he has learned." "Be with Kendra's dear son and help him feel your peace as he takes this test."

As their precious, caring words poured out, all I could think of was my own selfish nature. "How could I ask for prayer for a *test* when Carol's son will wake up this morning and the next and the next in a prison cell in Florida? What was I thinking? I am a poor excuse for a friend. This is so awful. Lord, how could I be so selfish?"

Those were my thoughts, and they completely controlled me. I could not wait for "amen" to come from the lips of my friends. "How much longer will they pray?" As I asked myself that question, they concluded, "In Jesus' name, amen." They stopped speaking, and I began.

"Oh, that's silly. It's really no big deal. It's just a test." I rambled on for about fifteen seconds until Carol interrupted me. "I know why you're saying that, Kendra. You are uncomfortable because we all know that J. P. is in prison for the rest of his life with no chance of parole. But there is something you *need* to know and understand. You are my friend. I love you, and because I love you, I love Jonathan and want him to do his very best on this exam."

*   *   *

You can give without loving,

but you cannot love without giving.

Amy Carmichael

*   *   *

That was it. Carol had said it all. That day Carol was an answer to prayer in so many ways. The most obvious way was in her heartfelt prayers for my son. She also understood my conflicted feelings. And beyond that she was a living illustration, an answer to my request made a day before: "Please Lord, show me what it looks like to be a generous friend."

*   *   *

It is more blessed to give than to receive.

Acts 20:35

*   *   *

Carol could have chosen to withhold her love, her prayers, and her generous friendship. If only her son was not confined to a prison for the rest of his natural life. If only the judge and jury had understood the overriding, innate discipline of a young naval officer who was trying to protect his vulnerable step-daughters. If only they had shown mercy.

But Carol chose not to live in her "if onlys." Instead she chose to be a generous friend—generous with love, generous with kindness, generous with encouragement. I can think of occasions when I have failed to be generous and have allowed

116

circumstances, the "if onlys" and "what ifs" of life, to control my words and actions. There have been too many times when I've thought of myself instead of others.

* * *

Let me live my life so that those to whom love is
a stranger will find in me a generous friend.
Robert Benson

* * *

If you can relate to my testimonial of failure more closely than you relate to the account of Carol's victory over her circumstances, do not dismay. She would be among the first to tell you that making the choice to love as Christ loves, to focus on others' needs, to give generously is a process. She writes, "Gene [her husband] and I realized we had to make a choice every day. Would we give in to despair and depression, or would we go on living a productive life, serving Christ? Would we quit ministry or would we continue to declare that God is good and He is trustworthy?"[9]

Yes, every day is a choice. That is true for Carol, and it is true for me and for you. Perhaps rather than *human beings* we should be called "human becomings." "Until we all reach unity in the faith and in the knowledge of the Son of God and become mature, attaining to the whole measure of the fullness of Christ (Ephesians 4:13).

* * *

First, give yourself to God.
You may be sure He'll look after what is His.
Author Unknown

* * *

The Christian walk is just that. It is a walk, not a sprint. Sometimes the path we travel is smooth and the walk is effortless. Sometimes the path is so rough, so formidable, with conditions so unbearable that the trek seems impossible. But as believers we know that is not the truth for we never walk alone.

Carol writes about taking her struggle to God, the only source of comfort:

> I found myself angry, often hurt, always broken—but the bottom line of my heart was this: Lord, where would I go if I turned away from You? If I didn't have You I would have nothing. I have nowhere to turn, so while I'm pounding Your chest with my hurt, pain, and anger, please know that I am still facing You, still leaning into the warmth of Your embrace, not sure I can trust You, but knowing You are all I have. If I left You, I would be completely aimless and lost. So while I feel devastated by what You have allowed to happen, I still cannot resist pressing into the comfort of Your strong arms. I am angry that I am not resisting You more, because I know You could have stopped this thing from happening—but I have nowhere else to go.[10]

The encounter I had with Carol, a generous friend, continues to encourage and inspire me to become more generous. My motivation is twofold. The most obvious is my desire to follow the Lord's instruction. And truthfully, it is also because I believe that being a generous friend to others will result in having generous friendships.

✳   ✳   ✳

I expect to pass through life but once.
If therefore, there be any kindness I can show, or any good
thing I can do to any fellow being, let me do it now,
and not defer or neglect it, as I shall not pass this way again.

William Penn

✳   ✳   ✳

CHOOSE TO
Reflect

Many times we think of generosity in terms of financial giving. The Word of God is calling us to be generous with more than our money. His desire is for each one of us to share out of the abundance He has provided. We are to give of our time, our talents, our encouragement, our enthusiasm, and our finances.

Giving generously is a privilege, and it has amazing results in God's economy: "Give, and it will be given to you. A good measure, pressed down, shaken together and running over, will be poured into your lap. For with the measure you use, it will be measured to you" (Luke 6:37–38). That incredible promise from God is not why we give generously; it is simply the supernatural result.

STUDY QUESTIONS

Choose Generosity

1. Remember the prayer "Let me live my life so that those to whom love is a stranger will find in me a generous friend." Is there someone in your life today who might be in need of a generous friend? What might you do to extend love to that person?

2. Can you give an example of a time when you had a need that was met by someone extending generous friendship? How does John 15:13 challenge you in this area?

3. What things keep you from becoming a generous friend?

4. God's Word tells us He loves a cheerful giver (2 Corinthians 9:7). Why do you think He encourages that attitude?

5. Name several ways you can give generously out of the abundance God has given you.

9
CHOOSE TO DREAM

*God can do anything, you know—far
more than you could ever imagine or guess
or request in your wildest dreams! He does
it not by pushing us around but by
working within us, his Spirit deeply and
gently within us.*

EPHESIANS 3:20, The Message

Evelina had dreams—dreams beyond what might have been considered reasonable for the daughter of two migrant workers and the granddaughter of Mexican emigrants. Her heritage had a strong impact on her, not with its limitations but with the dreams of what was possible.

Although her parents met as migrant workers in the sweet cornfields of Illinois and Texas, they decided to raise their family in a more permanent location. They chose a rural community in central Illinois. Ramon and Maria wanted a stable home and community for their children.

It was soon obvious that being one of the few Mexican families in a small town in Illinois would not be easy. There was discrimination and racial bias to overcome. Evelina's parents did not allow those negative circumstances to destroy their dream. They were determined to become woven into the fabric of the community in a positive way. Evelina's father found employment in a nearby city, working at a General Motors foundry. Her mother was an at-home mom. Together Ramon and Maria encouraged and inspired their children to dream big, and the dreaming started at an early age.

When Evelina was only six years old her dream starting taking shape. She told anyone who would listen that she was "going to be 'in' the TV" when she grew up. In junior high she created a checklist of the one hundred things she wanted to do before she died. In the small high school she attended she was involved in almost every extracurricular activity offered to young women. She was a high achiever in all areas—in academics, in music, and in relationships. The delightful, young go-getter was well on her way to achieving her dreams!

*   *   *

Now faith is confidence in what we hope for

and assurance about what we do not see.

Hebrews 11:1

*   *   *

Evelina was filled with hope and with the faith instilled in her as a child. Even though she could not see the path she would travel, she felt ready for the adventure. After high school Evelina entered college—something neither her parents nor grandparents had been privileged to do. She began to check things off that bucket list she had written a few years before.

With each item accomplished she had a clearer picture of her dream and became more motivated to start living that dream. She was certain that "God can do anything, you know—far more than you could ever imagine or guess or request in your wildest dreams!" (Ephesians 3:20, The Message).

Evelina graduated from college in only three years. She was strikingly beautiful, a hard-charger with a bachelor of arts degree in both broadcast journalism and media and Spanish. Soon after graduation she received a paid-in-full fellowship from the International Radio and Television Society Foundation and moved to New York City to accept the dream job. This remarkable assignment held the potential to open many doors for Evelina. She chose to cover entertainment news and spent an incredible summer doing just that in New York City. The future seemed bright with all Evelina's dreams coming together. But things are not always as they seem.

* * *

Be very careful, then, how you live—not as unwise

but as wise, making the most of every opportunity,

because the days are evil.

Ephesians 5:15–16

* * *

Evelina and countless others found their plans abruptly interrupted on September 11, 2001. It is safe to say that the tragedy of 9/11 was a shock and surprise to everyone. It was also an unmistakable life-changer. Although Evelina was on assignment in Los Angeles and not home in New York City, the destruction of the twin towers had its effect.

The show Evelina hoped would be the next step in the pursuit of her dreams had been canceled, and media jobs were no longer available to young, aspiring talent. New York City was reeling from the attacks, and recovery would take time.

Initially Evelina felt as if her dream had died. Then she took time to step back and gain perspective. "I realized that circumstances cannot determine my future. That is up to the Lord. Circumstances are only temporary."

*　　*　　*

Far away there in the sunshine are my highest aspirations.
I may not reach them, but I can look up and see their beauty,
believe in them, and try to follow where they lead.
Louisa May Alcott

*　　*　　*

Evelina's dreams and plans had been altered, but they had not been erased. After a time of regrouping, she joined the staff of the University of Miami as the Assistant Director of Multicultural Affairs. In addition, she worked with the presidential debates on campus, MTV Video Music awards, and Teen Choice Awards for Latino youth.

As if all that were not enough, Evelina began training for a marathon. It was in the midst of this busy schedule that her life's plans were changed in a monumental way—in a way no one could have ever predicted.

*　　*　　*

We are all faced with a series of great opportunities
brilliantly disguised as impossible situations.
Chuck Swindoll

*　　*　　*

One morning Evelina woke up with a bruise on her left calf. It seemed to have come from nowhere. That bruise, first just the size of a dime, grew. Within two weeks it was the size of a softball and there were other signs that something was wrong. Although she went to the doctor several times, the physician showed very little concern. Because of that, Evelina decided she did not need to be concerned. That attitude was sufficient for a while—until the day she began having chest pains and developed a fever. Then Evelina's roommate rushed her to the hospital.

The diagnosis was a pulmonary embolism. The blood clot that had formed in her calf weeks before had traveled to her lungs. Pulmonary embolisms are the third most common cause of death in the United States. Although she suffered permanent damage to her lungs, Evelina's life was spared, and just as important, her focus was adjusted. She did not stop dreaming; she simply honed her vision for the future, trying to be certain it lined up with the Lord's desire for her life. "Through the lengthy hospitalization and rehabilitation program," writes Evelina, "I begged God to help me find the strength to handle the challenge. Ultimately, I did a lot of journaling and was forced to reexamine my life and priorities and pinpoint what I truly valued."[11]

Evelina turned to the Lord for strength. Where had she learned about this source of peace and power? As a child she attended church regularly at a church where God was revered but the gospel message was not taught. By the time she reached junior high school, she found herself surrounded by committed Christian friends. Relationships like these continued into high school, college, and beyond. It was this parade of loving friends who helped her understand that faith is more than regularly attending worship services. Faith involves a personal relationship with Christ. Her peers were prepared to "give the reason for the hope" they had within them (1 Peter 3:15), and Evelina began to build a personal relationship with her heavenly Father. Years later as she and I talked together, her words reflected her understanding: "Growing up I had a great deal of religion, but not much relationship." That can be a problem in any setting or denomination.

It was Evelina's growing relationship with Christ that gave her the courage not to give up but to cry out to God. She refused to live in her "if onlys." If only she had not developed a pulmonary embolism, she could be pursuing her dream. If only the doctors had diagnosed it sooner, the embolism might not have done as much damage.

No "if onlys" for Evelina! Instead she looked forward to the life she could enjoy as soon as she was able. She had faith to look beyond the temporary though painful setback and to look forward to the dream she believed the Lord had given her. Evelina had no reason to suspect that her faith would be tested very soon and that she would realize with much more intensity the importance of continually strengthening her relationship with Christ.

*   *   *

You can have all this world, but give me Jesus.
Traditional spiritual

*   *   *

When Evelina had recovered sufficiently from the pulmonary embolism, she made another change in location. She joined the staff at the University of Texas as a Student Affairs Administrator. Her parents were now living in Texas, so the relocation was advantageous from every standpoint. Although this was a positive move, Evelina felt the Lord was calling her to take a different path, one where the miracles she had experienced would inspire others and bring God glory. Evelina launched Sol2Soul and made a commitment to go and speak wherever God sent her: "My vision was to engage, enlighten, empower, and entertain my audience in order for them to discover and live their true life's purpose. My dream was to teach people how to identify and build on their talents, thus developing their talents into strengths in order to achieve maximum potential in the classroom, home and/or workplace. My hope was that these individuals would create a chain reaction that would impact others and thus leave this world a better place than they found it."[12]

Evelina became a certified academic/life coach and left her position at the University of Texas. It seemed that the time had come to capture her dream. She was completely unaware that the dream would once again be changed by circumstances beyond her control.

*   *   *

Your worst days are never so bad that you are beyond the reach of God's grace. And your best days are never so good that you're beyond the need of God's grace.
Jerry Bridges

*   *   *

Evelina went for an annual routine checkup, and it turned out to be anything but routine. After several additional tests, she was diagnosed with two incurable and rare autoimmune diseases. She underwent sixteen blood transfusions. Her body was not producing enough platelets, and her blood was not clotting. Because of that, even the most seemingly insignificant wounds could not heal. Ultimately Evelina's spleen was removed. The days were not easy as she recovered from this drastic surgery, and some days were more difficult than others.

A year later, Evelina was hospitalized once again with complications from lupus. During that time she suffered three seizures in a week, and at one point her heart stopped beating. "In spite of the situation, we all kept our faith and relied totally on God for comfort, peace, and healing," she explains. "After waking up in ICU two weeks after I had been admitted,

I found myself not able to walk, talk or even eat. My doctors told my parents that we'd be lucky if I was able to walk within a year. In addition, the medical staff informed me that I would be in chemotherapy for six months following my hospitalization. I had no idea the amount of pain and swelling I would endure and all the physical changes my body would end up going through. Losing almost all of my hair and retaining water throughout my body made me realize that vanity is the first thing to go when you are struck with an illness."[13]

At that point Evelina had fewer skills than a two-year-old. Her young body had been ravaged.

* * *

The journey of a thousand miles starts with a single step.

Chinese proverb

* * *

It had to feel like a thousand-mile journey for Evelina. She had to wonder if she would ever be able even to take the first step to begin the journey.

Why was this happening to her? Why did she have to endure such an enormous setback—a setback that might be permanent? Even though the question of "Why?" was one Evy asked initially, she realized she might never know the answer.

The "Why?" questions asked in the midst of pain or trial seldom have an answer. Perhaps the more important questions begin with the word "What?" What can I learn from these circumstances? What am I able to teach others? What would the Lord have me do? What is the next right choice? The answers to *those* questions are more likely to surface. Asking "Why?" is akin to living in the futility of the "if onlys" and "what ifs." They cannot change the situation, nor can they advance the cause of Christ.

So Evelina asked, "What?" and knew her next course of

action. It was to go through intensive therapy—speech therapy, physical therapy, occupational therapy, and most important, spiritual therapy. Evelina's body may have been ravaged, but her faith was strong and growing stronger. She was certain the Lord wanted her to regain her abilities. Not surprising, she approached that challenge with all she had.

Evelina may have initially had difficulty walking, but she was running to the throne of God: "In him and through faith in him we may approach God with freedom and confidence" (Ephesians 3:12). Evelina's battle was not over. She could have given up on her dreams, the dreams the Lord was directing. Very few would have blamed her for quitting. But instead she persevered with confidence in the One who loved her best.

* * *

A child can ask questions that a wise man cannot answer.

Author unknown

* * *

My children and I sat around the small table in the kitchen. My husband, John, had gone to work before the sun came up, and the boys had just finished eating their cereal. I opened up the *Bible in Pictures for Little Eyes* for our morning devotions. The story for the day was about Peter walking on the water (Matthew 14:25–30).

You know how it goes: The disciples were in a boat on the lake. It was right before dawn, and they saw a terrifying sight. A figure was coming toward them, walking on the water. In fear they cried out, "It's a ghost." But then they heard a familiar voice in reply. It was Jesus coming their way. He responded by simply saying, "Take courage! It is I. Don't be afraid."

Peter, always the impetuous one, sounded back, "Lord, if it's you, tell me to come to you on the water." When Jesus responded, "Come," Peter hopped out of the boat without reservation.

Lo and behold, Peter was walking on the water too—at least at first. Matthew 14:30 sums up Peter's short trek and his soggy finish. "But when he saw the wind, he was afraid and, beginning to sink, cried out, "Lord, save me!"

The Bible story for the day ended at that point. I was preparing to pray when my eldest son interrupted with an interesting declaration: "I know why Peter sank!"

It was difficult to imagine how my son could possibly make a claim like that. He had never studied theology. He had never formally studied anything; he was only four years old. Surely one needed credentials to address the issue of a sinking apostle.

Determined that it would be an interesting exchange, I encouraged him to continue. "You do? Okay, why did Peter sink?"

"That's easy! He quit lookin' at Jesus!"

After a moment of reflection, I realized he was 100 percent accurate. Peter sank when he "regarded the wind and the waves." He sank when he "quit lookin' at Jesus."

Evelina did not quit lookin' at Jesus. She kept her faith, her hope, her confidence, and her dreams strong by keeping her eyes on Him.

*　　*　　*

"For I know the plans I have for you," declares the Lord,

"plans to prosper you and not to harm you,

plans to give you hope and a future."

Jeremiah 29:11

*　　*　　*

The message of Jeremiah 29:11 is comforting and reassuring. Occasionally it is also misunderstood. The tendency is to read that promise of God and then determine precisely what the future will bring. Take note that the Word says, "the plans

I have for you." The Lord is not promising He'll follow *your* plans. This is where faith is crucial. When we "take delight in the Lord, He gives us the desires of our hearts" (Psalm 37:4). Our desires and dreams are assured because they are aligned with the Lord's desires for us.

It is amazing how often we imagine that we know what the days and weeks ahead will hold. We have our day planners and smart phones, and we assume that a quick look at our calendars will let us know what to expect.

The truth is that each day has an unknown element whether or not we recognize it. You and I and my friend Evelina can't assume that our plans for the day will come to pass. They may and they may not. But as we are faithful, God's plans for us will be fulfilled.

The Lord gave Evelina the dream He wanted her to have, and He gave her the strength to live that dream in spite of overwhelming circumstances. She did not underestimate nor fail to appreciate what God had done for her. The gift of life is often taken for granted, but not so often by someone who has had a brush with death.

*　　　*　　　*

**But since you excel in everything—in faith,
in speech, in knowledge, in complete earnestness
and in the love we have kindled in you—
see that you also excel in this grace of giving.**
2 Corinthians 8:7

*　　　*　　　*

Evelina's dream is the living illustration of "excelling in everything," especially in the love God had kindled in her. She left her stable job at the University of Texas to go on the road speaking at schools, colleges, and churches—anywhere there was hunger for the message God had given her. Evelina is a survivor. Her circumstances do not hold her back. The victory belongs to the Lord!

Evelina's mission today is to bring the message of faith and hope to others. "It is clear to me that we have two choices: We can either change the world or be changed by the world. You can either live for a greater purpose, or live for yourself. None of us is guaranteed tomorrow, so we must use our God-given gifts and talents right now."

Evelina survived a journey none of us would want to take. She was not alone on that journey but was holding the hand of God. Her family was also with her every step of the way, praying for her, encouraging her, and helping her overcome the trauma her body and mind had experienced.

Evelina did not give up on her dreams. She simply allowed the Lord to shape and mold them so His purpose was fulfilled.

One of her dreams recently came to pass. She and Ivan Castellon, an army veteran, have become husband and wife! Ivan was awarded two purple hearts in service to his country and, in the words of Evelina, "He is kind and loving and understands physical problems and rehabilitation more than most folks do. That means he also understands my life. God is so amazing to bring us together. His plan is perfect!"

The gift of life is often taken for granted and so is the gift of a loving mate, but not as often by someone who has had a brush with death or imagined they would never find the one with whom they could share their life.

*　　*　　*

For many are invited, but few are chosen.
Matthew 22:14

*　　*　　*

"I know God has chosen me, because of the extraordinary health situations I have gone through and the unconditional love and compassion He's given me for people. For this reason, it is in my heart and soul to lift up the name of Jesus!" says Evelyn. "Life is all about being used as an instrument in the hands of our God Almighty. It's about Jesus giving His life for our sins. I am an ordinary person who has been able to overcome extraordinary health situations all with the help of God."

I could not have said it better. Evelina is the real deal. She has been a part of my life for close to twenty years, and it is a joy for me to introduce you to this woman whose faith is in Jesus and whose dreams are rightly placed—in His hands!

CHOOSE TO
Reflect

Romans 5:3–5 says, "Not only so, but we also glory in our sufferings, because we know that suffering produces perseverance; perseverance, character; and character, hope. And hope does not put us to shame, because God's love has been poured out into our hearts through the Holy Spirit, who has been given to us."

Sufferings are not pleasant. They are just as the name suggests—circumstances that cause us to suffer or feel pain. These circumstances, though unwelcome, are inevitable. This passage of Scripture suggests we are to see the positive chain of events that can occur as we suffer for Christ: our sufferings—then perseverance— followed by character—and finally hope, shameless amazing hope covered by God's unfailing love. What cause for joy!

STUDY QUESTIONS

Choose to Dream

1. When did something you had hoped for fail to come to pass? In hindsight do you feel disappointment, or can you see wisdom in the outcome?

2. Have you allowed an "if only" or "what if" to destroy your dream?

3. Does your life today resemble the one you anticipated as a young woman? If not, how is it different?

4. Share about a time when you were surprised by God's miraculous action or provision.

5. Is there an "if only" or "what if" you are facing right now?

10

CHOOSE
TO HOPE

See, he's not just anyone. He's my son.

MARK SCHULTZ

The words of the Mark Schultz song rang in Lynne's ears. She began praying, pleading that what she was hearing was incorrect. She was hoping God would intervene in a mighty way in the life of her son, a son who had just been diagnosed with Duchenne muscular dystrophy. Everett was only three at the time. Even though the diagnosis was devastating, it was not surprising. For about six months Lynne had suspected she would hear those fateful words from a physician.

What made her suspect that her little boy would soon be diagnosed with muscular dystrophy? Lynne was already familiar with the disease. Her younger brother had died as the result of muscular dystrophy when he was only a teenager. He had suffered from the same disease that now plagued her firstborn child.

Duchenne muscular dystrophy is an inherited disorder involving rapidly progressive muscle weakness. It is caused by a defective gene passed from mother to son. Because of Lynne's experience, she recognized the symptoms before the official diagnosis was made. "One day I saw Everett going up the stairs, and he was putting his hand on his knee and pushing down to help himself up to the next step. I had seen that same thing years ago when my brother, in the early stages of muscular dystrophy, climbed the stairs in our parents' home." Her son's symptoms had begun to show.

*　　　*　　　*

Let us hold unswervingly to the hope we profess,
for he who promised is faithful.
Hebrews 10:23

*　　　*　　　*

Because of Lynne's firsthand knowledge of muscular dystrophy, the things she hoped for might not have been as extravagant as a parent with less experience with the disease, a parent like her husband, Everett's dad. He wanted to believe something more optimistic than the stark reality. Facing the truth of the diagnosis and prognosis was very difficult for him. It was easier to be in denial. This turn of events combined with other factors put a great strain on their marriage.

Lynne and her husband had met in graduate school, both studying linguistics and hoping to serve as Bible translators. After graduation they were married and left for the mission field together. Everett was born in Thailand. Shortly after his birth, the family returned to the states, where they served at the home office for their mission board.

Lynne was pregnant again. If a second son had been conceived, there was a 50/50 change he would have muscular dystrophy. Lynne's older sister had three sons, and none of them had the disease. That gave Lynne and her husband confidence as she carried her second child.

About two years after Everett was born, Lynne gave birth to Austin, her second son. By the time he was eighteen months old, they discovered that he also had muscular dystrophy. This compounded the problems Lynne and her husband were facing in their marriage. She turned to the Lord for strength and guidance in the difficult situation. He turned to addictive behaviors. Eventually, their marriage ended.

*   *   *

Waste not fresh tears over old griefs.

Euripides

*   *   *

Picture this: Lynne is newly divorced. She is a single mom who must support herself and her two sons, both of whom have muscular dystrophy. They need specialized medical and personal care, and she is living in Texas, two thousand miles from her extended family.

It seemed sensible—and necessary for survival—to move back home to Minnesota. There she would receive both practical and emotional help. If there was anyone who could understand her situation, it was her own mother. "My ex-husband taunted me, saying I would never be able to survive. I didn't argue with him. I just knew he was wrong. God would take care of us!"

Lynne and the boys moved to Minnesota to start a new life. But the move was not as smooth as she would have liked. The worst of it was the attitude that Austin developed. As Lynne once said, "He was going through some sort of teenage rebellion about five years too early."

*   *   *

Get rid of all bitterness, rage and anger,
brawling and slander,
along with every form of malice.
Ephesians 4:31

*   *   *

Austin was angry about the move to Minnesota and equally, if not more, angry about the divorce. He saw everything as Lynne's fault. Symptoms of his muscular dystrophy were beginning to surface, and he was no longer able to keep up with the other kids. Even at that young age, he understood that Lynne was the carrier of the disease. This fueled his negative feelings toward her.

To punish his mother Austin would tell Lynne he was going to hurt himself and that he wished he had never been born. He also threatened to hurt Lynne.

*   *   *

The Lord disciplines the one he loves,
and he chastens everyone he accepts as his son.
Hebrews 12:6

*   *   *

The divorce and the move had not only taken its toll on Austin. Lynne's feelings were also ragged. She was exhausted, physically and emotionally, and knew something needed to change. "When Austin started acting out his negative feelings, I realized I hadn't been very consistent with discipline. I needed help to discover consequences I could establish that would make a difference and to learn how to give positive reinforcement for good behavior. I did not want to raise a child who was forever suicidal and dangerous."

Counseling helped Lynne develop creative ways to encourage good behavior, to set adequate, loving consequences, and to follow through with them. With the Lord as her model, she understood the need to lovingly discipline her sons. She was both father and mother to them, and she wanted them to understand how much she loved them both. That love included discipline.

Over and over as Lynne was both delivering consequences for boundaries that had been crossed and as she was rewarding good behavior, she would share with her sons about her motivation—why she was doing what she was doing. She told the boys she wanted them to have a good life with good friends. She would tell that she wanted them to achieve all they could achieve. She wanted things to go well for them.

Ultimately the boys understood that Lynne was not disciplining them because she was angry or frustrated. She was on their side, wanting them to succeed. "Another big reason I was parenting with discipline was because I had to answer to God for how I raised my children, and I was submitting to God's authority—the ultimate authority I wanted for my sons." Lynne had to be consistent and enforce the consequences motivated by love and obedience to God. The change in her discipline strategy resulted in positive change in both Austin and Everett's attitudes and actions.

*   *   *

I do not understand what I do.

For what I want to do I do not do, but what I hate I do.

Romans 7:15

*   *   *

One of the very last outbursts of Austin's anger was directed differently from the ones Lynne had seen earlier. Austin was angry not with Lynne, but with himself. The frustration he felt had been mounting as he realized he was repeatedly making mistakes he did not want to make: "I *can't* do the right thing! I want to and I try, but I still do the wrong things so many times." How similar Austin's words were to those of the apostle Paul in Romans 7.

No one can always do the right thing. Or as the Scripture states, "All have sinned and fall short of the glory of God" (Romans 3:23).

God used Austin's angry outburst, and a single mom's hope and prayers were answered. Austin accepted Christ, something Everett had done already. The gospel message had come alive to both of Lynne's sons.

As Everett's and Austin's illness progressed, the hope of heaven was reassuring to them and to Lynne. In heaven their bodies would be whole. They would have no sickness or pain and they would be able to walk and run and dance before the throne of God!

*   *   *

All the world is full of suffering.
It is also full of overcoming.
Helen Keller

*   *   *

Lynne's bachelor's degree was in art with a minor in music. Before she and the boys moved from Texas to Minnesota, she had been working with another artist, using her talent to paint murals in several homes in affluent Dallas neighborhoods. She enjoyed what she did and hoped somehow to be able to use her talent and experience to secure similar work when she relocated. Unfortunately she was unable to discover any established businesses that could use her art background. As a result Lynne decided to strike out on her own. Although her business was successful, she quickly learned that it was very difficult to balance the demands she faced as the single mother of two sons with special needs and the demands of managing her own business.

Lynne's problems were very real. How could she support her family and care for her sons? How could she make a living and a life for Everett and Austin? It was a struggle, and Lynne searched for God's guidance, holding onto hope and yet knowing the challenges would only continue to increase.

*   *   *

Courage is not the opposite of fear.

It is fear well placed.

Author unknown

*   *   *

Lynne knew the Lord would meet her family's needs because she had seen Him do that month after month. He provided food for their table and a roof over their heads—many times in a very creative way. Being self-employed was exhausting and took time away from the boys. Perhaps there was another way, a more creative way, the Lord could meet their needs.

*   *   *

Those who honor me I will honor.

1 Samuel 2:30

*   *   *

Lynne had an acquaintance who was being paid to be the caretaker for his own disabled son. There had been some deceit when the position was acquired. The arrangement was slightly underhanded, perhaps even illegal. Lynne imagined the great blessing it would be to be acknowledged and reimbursed as her sons' caregiver, but she also knew that a legally questionable path was not one she wanted to take. She feared that things would get more difficult as the boys got older, but more than that she feared being separated from the Lord by choosing to do something outside of His will.

Lynne shared her concerns and her hope with Everett and Austin's caseworker. Miraculously, the caseworker knew of a proper and legal way that Lynne could be appointed as the boys' caregiver. She applied for and received a grant. God had once again provided for the family.

*   *   *

You have to accept whatever comes, and the only important thing is that you meet it with courage and with the best you have to give.

Eleanor Roosevelt

*   *   *

Things were going pretty smoothly for Lynne and the boys. Everett and Austin were both in wheelchairs now, and their home had been made accessible. They were doing well in school and had developed some good friendships. Lynne was playing the violin in the community orchestra and leading a worship team at church. She was being fed by the Lord, literally and figuratively, physically and emotionally. And then the unspeakable happened. She and the boys were traveling home on a rainy day from her grandfather's ninety-fifth birthday party. The stoplight turned red as Lynne approached the intersection. Even while braking she realized she was not going to be able to stop in time. As her car skidded forward, it collided with the one that had already come to a stop. Lynne and Austin were shaken up, and even though Everett initially appeared to be unhurt, before long it was determined he had actually been seriously injured.

Everett's condition was critical, and the physicians could not determine why his body was filling with air. A surgical procedure became necessary to try to find the answers. As always,

Lynne was by his side. From her Caring Bridge journal she wrote, "It was very unsettling, and I was very tearful as I sat and talked to Everett just before his surgery. I understood that those could possibly be my last words to him. I told him things like, 'I'm so glad I get to be your mom. You're such a sweet boy. I came to sit by you for a little while. (He always asks me to sit by him.) Look to God. Just keep looking to God.'"

That surgery was just the beginning of a long time of recovery. The accident had occurred in early September and it would be December before Lynne would write these words:

> Everett came home from the hospital last Tuesday. He is doing well and gets in his chair more and more each day. He was up in it today for five hours. He enjoyed a good day playing video games and watching a DVD with a friend. He will start therapies and tutoring this coming week, so the relaxed recovery pace will definitely change. The cats love sitting with him on the bed. His care is quite involved, requiring two people to move him around. Mom and Dad have been a huge help. Mom has been staying overnight to help with turning him at night. He is back to eating normal amounts of normal food, so that will help him get better quickly. The biggest challenges are ahead as he learns new ways to perform certain tasks. Occupational therapy will be a big help there. He is in good spirits and pleasant. Much to be thankful for!
> —Lynne

*   *   *

**You cannot escape the responsibility
of tomorrow by evading it today.**
Abraham Lincoln

*   *   *

Lynne was no stranger to responsibility. In fact, she was the poster child for it. Everett's care became more demanding, and the realization that she may have been at fault in the accident was very sobering. Lynne blamed herself for all the suffering Everett had endured, and the guilt was almost overwhelming. "I haven't been a good mom!" Thoughts like that were filling her mind with guilt. "Life is really hard. If only I had a husband to help me. I'm so tired. I'm not taking good care of the boys. I don't have time for orchestra, Bible study group, exercising. I don't feel like cooking today." And on and on the thoughts raced through Lynne's mind. One day she realized she had gone ten days without washing her hair. At that point it was obvious to her that she was in depression.

Where was her hope? It was buried in her "if onlys" and "what ifs." If only she had a husband to care for her. If only the boys had a father who could give them love and guidance. If only finances weren't a stressor. If only her life wasn't so difficult. If only Everett hadn't been hurt so badly in the accident. What if he doesn't recover? What if she never gets more energy? What if she can't take care of the physical needs of her boys? What if she truly is a failure as a mom?

*   *   *

I found myself at the end of my rope,

and the only knot I had was Jesus.

Author unknown

*   *   *

As Lynne turned to the Lord in her desperation, He was quick to remind her of the things she *could* do and choices she could make. She chose to stop dwelling on the "if onlys" and the "what ifs" and look at what she began calling the "positive truths" in her life. As she looked at each thing that had discouraged her, she asked, "What is the positive truth in this?" and her hope began to return.

As a result she made some changes. She began to welcome more help with her boys. This eased her workload with her sons' care. She purposed to get to bed on time each night, to start exercising, and to get back into her weekly Bible study group. She even started playing in the community orchestra again. These things had been eliminated one by one in the false hope that their elimination would give her more time, more energy, and more enthusiasm for her daily tasks. What resulted instead was isolation and loneliness, amplifying her feelings of despair and depression.

*   *   *

I cannot change yesterday.

I can only make the most of today,

and look with hope to tomorrow.

Author unknown

*   *   *

The time Lynne spent in her "if onlys" was cut short by living in the truth. God's Word is very clear that the truth will set you free (John 8:32). Instead of believing the lies of the enemy, Lynne chose to hope and to live in the promises of God. He was able to supply her needs. He was able to give her wisdom as a parent. He would never leave her nor forsake her.

Lynne has hope for her tomorrow and the tomorrow for her sons. "We have fun thinking and dreaming about what they will be able to do in heaven. Austin in particular is looking forward to running for all he is worth and then jumping into the air."

I wonder. Will he be jumping into the arms of Jesus?

CHOOSE TO
Reflect

1 Thessalonians 4:13–14 says, "Brothers and sisters, we do not want you to be uninformed about those who sleep in death, so that you do not grieve like the rest of mankind, who have no hope. For we believe that Jesus died and rose again, and so we believe that God will bring with Jesus those who have fallen asleep in him." Imagine what heaven will look like, feel like, be like. Imagine living eternally in the presence of your heavenly Father, who is love. Nothing could be any better than that!

STUDY QUESTIONS

Choose to Hope

1. Lynne's situation is difficult to fathom. Can you share about a time when your circumstances felt overwhelming?

2. What were the "if onlys" associated with that situation? Were there "what ifs" you had to overcome?

3. What discouragement are you facing today? Examine that discouragement, and name the "positive truth" of the situation that you can choose to emphasize.

4. What is something you hope for? In whom is your hope placed?

11

CHOOSE JESUS

There is no pit so deep that Jesus
is not deeper still.

CORRIE TEN BOOM

I had volunteered to work at a Christian book booth at the Illinois State Fair for three days. As I worked, I began to wonder why I had done this. It must have been a weak moment, or maybe I had forgotten what August was like in central Illinois. Working the state fair was not a prime assignment. The temperature each day was between eighty and ninety-five degrees, and the humidity equaled the temperature. The old building that housed the exhibits was not air-conditioned, so at the end of each thirteen-hour day we had to lay the books flat so their covers would not curl up completely. Each morning we turned the books around again for display.

As I reorganized my book display on the last day of my assignment, someone interrupted my work.

"Kendra?" the woman's voice questioned. "Is that you?"

I turned around to see Jill, a childhood friend, standing at the edge of the booth. Her family had lived next door to my family when we were growing up. Jill's younger sister, Jane, had been my best friend from age four until we left for college. At that time our lives went in two different directions.

As the "older sister," Jill had to put up with a lot from us. We were typical younger brats. We faithfully monitored her boyfriends' calls; cast her in all the rotten parts in the plays we wrote, directed, produced, and starred in; bugged her while her friends were visiting her, and so on. You get the picture. She was easygoing and put up with us way beyond what was expected.

Jane and I were not only notorious "little sisters" to Jill, but for many years we were also inseparable best friends.

*   *   *

Friendship is the greatest of worldly goods.

Certainly to me it is the chief happiness of life.

C. S. Lewis

*   *   *

In the summer months Jane and I ate almost every lunch together. Our moms even allowed us to eat the main course at one home and the dessert at the other. We'd check the menus at each house, then declare our culinary itinerary.

We walked, biked, and eventually drove to school together almost every day for thirteen years and had the same teachers from kindergarten through sixth grade. My birthday is on February 22. At the beginning of February when Jane and I were in the first grade, our teacher was giving an overview of the coming events. There was Valentine's Day, she told us, and the birthdays of two important people.

"Do any of you know who they are?" asked our teacher.

Someone identified Abraham Lincoln almost immediately,

but we all struggled to think of the other important person. Then suddenly Jane's hand shot into the air.

"Yes?" asked our teacher.

"Kendra was born in February," Jane said proudly.

The fact that she believed she'd accurately identified an important person born in February and solved the teacher's riddle gives you a picture of our friendship. Where Jane was, Kendra was. Where Kendra was, Jane was, and whenever possible we both tagged along with Jill.

That was thirty years before the August meeting at the book booth on the fairgrounds. Many things had changed over those years.

Jill went to college first, and three years later Jane and I followed. From that point on, our lives did not intersect often. Upon graduating, Jill worked in Chicago, where she discovered *The Living Bible,* the Moody Bible Institute, and Jesus (in that order). As a young adult I discovered John (my best friend and husband), marriage, and Jesus. Jill and I had a new bond, a great bond, which had not existed before. We both loved Jesus. Jane had discovered many things also—but she had not found Jesus.

I dreamed about sharing my faith with my childhood friend. I imagined what I would say to her and how she would respond. Every time I heard the song "Pass It On," I internalized the words in the last verse and thought of Jane. I wished for Jane the happiness that I'd found. I wanted to shout to her that the Lord of love had come into my life. I'd sing the chorus with great gusto as I thought about Jane.

But I didn't—pass it on, that is. "What if" I shared the gospel message with Jan and she became angry with me or rejected my friendship? We'd see one another at Christmas and relive our childhood memories. We'd spend time reminiscing and remembering the fun of the past. Jill and I would keep relatively quiet about our faith. At those holiday reunions we could have talked for hours, maybe even days, about the love we shared for Jesus, but it just wasn't feasible.

That's why the fairground meeting with Jill was wonderful! It was a surprise meeting—a splendid serendipity.

"What are you doing here?" I asked Jill.

"My roommate, Barb, and I brought her niece to the fair to enter the pigtail contest," Jill explained.

A glance at the long braids confirmed that she was definitely a contender.

"I'm here for one more day, selling Christian books," I told her. "Someone relieves me tonight. This is such a treat! Tell me, what's new? How is your job? Your family?" I asked hurriedly. "How are your mom and dad? And Jane and Jay and little Holly?"

"Hold on," Jill laughed. "One thing at a time. Mom and Dad are doing well."

"You look just like your beautiful mom," I interrupted, suddenly overwhelmed by the similarity and by the subtle passing of time. "And Jane? How is Jane?"

"She's really enjoying being a mom. She's busy and doing pretty well," Jill answered.

"Does she know Jesus?" I inquired.

"Not yet," Jill answered, "but with both of us praying, it is just a matter of time."

"What is Jesus doing in your life?" I asked.

Then we began to share our deepest thoughts concerning our love for the Savior.

The next thirty minutes were wonderful. It was the highlight of my state fair experience. After Jill left the booth that morning, I knew beyond question that this had not been a chance meeting but that God had blessed me with an encounter *He* had arranged.

The next day was even stickier and hotter. It was the sauna-like kind of day that appeals only to the corn growing in the fields. It has been said that on steamy August days, if you stand completely still, you can hear the corn grow. Jill wasn't listening to the corn that day. She and Barb, Barb's mom, sister, and niece were all settled in an air-conditioned car, traveling the Illinois country roads.

*   *   *

All I have seen teaches me to trust
the Creator for all I have not seen.
Ralph Waldo Emerson

*   *   *

Jill was sitting in the backseat with her roommate's mom as the car navigated the lonely back roads, hemmed in tightly by the gently swaying corn. Country roads are beautiful on a late summer day, but that beauty can be deceptive. The mature corn plants are tall and leafy and can serve as screens blocking intersections—screens that can mask oncoming cars. That is precisely what happened.

As the car carrying my friend Jill slowed and moved into a blind intersection, an oncoming car from the left could not be avoided. Neither car was able to stop. The next moment had to be one of shock and terror as the two cars collided. The point of impact was the back door of the car. Jill was killed, and so was Barb's mother.

My phone rang that afternoon after I got home from the fair.

"There was a car accident a few hours ago," said a woman who had grown up in our little town. "Jill was killed. The officials have already called her sister, Jane. I thought you might not know yet."

"I just saw Jill yesterday," I exclaimed, as though our encounter should somehow have exempted her from harm.

"That's wonderful!" the woman replied. "That might be a comfort to Jane."

The conversation ended, and I immediately dialed Jane's

number. "Jane, I just heard about Jill. I'm so sorry!" I sobbed. Jane was crying too.

"Jane," I continued, "I just saw Jill yesterday. We were both at the Illinois State Fair. We spent about half an hour talking together!"

"Oh," Jane cried, "I want you to tell me every word. We are on our way home now. It'll take about four hours. Can you meet me at my parents' house?"

"I'll be there when you arrive," I said. "I love you." As I hung up the phone, I turned her words over again and again in my mind. Jane had said, "I want you to tell me every word." "Lord," I prayed, "help me to remember and recount every word."

*   *   *

Carry each other's burdens, and in this

way you will fulfill the law of Christ.

Galatians 6:2

*   *   *

By 3:30 I was waiting in Jane's parents' living room. Moments later Jane arrived. The car pulled up to the house, and she rushed inside. Jane and her husband and baby girl were comforted by the many friends who were together. She and I hugged and cried, and finally we stole away to the bedroom to be alone.

"Tell me everything Jill said," Jane begged. "Tell me your whole conversation."

I had been reconstructing the conversation in my mind for the last four hours, and now I replayed the entire thing as accurately as I could.

"We talked about Jill's job," I said, "and about your folks. We talked about how sweet your little girl is. We talked about books we'd read, were reading, and wanted to read. And most importantly, we talked about Jesus! In fact," I continued, "that is who we talked about most of the time."

I explained to Jane how important Jesus was to both of us. I told her that He was the most important person in Jill's life.

Jane listened intently and constantly encouraged me to continue. When I finally could remember no other piece of conversation, I stopped.

Jane looked at me and said quite simply, "I want to be a Christian. Tell me what to do."

God's Word tells us always to be prepared to give an answer for the hope within us (see 1 Peter 3:15). It is for moments like this that we memorize the four spiritual laws. It's moments like this that we imagine as we pray for loved ones.

As coherently as possible, I shared the gospel with Jane. I told her that God loved her and had a wonderful plan for her life. I told her all of us were sinful and that it was this sin that separated us from God. The sin created a huge gulf between God and us. I told her that Jesus was the bridge over this separation, that He died in our place and rose again. I told her that He was the only way to God. I told Jane that every person had to accept Christ personally, just as her sister Jill had done, in order to know God's love.

When I finished the explanation, we prayed together and Jane received Christ as her Savior.

"It's just like the little booklet I read this afternoon," she exclaimed excitedly.

"What?" I asked, completely confused.

"The little booklet. Wait, I'll show you. It's here in my pocket."

Jane reached into her pocket and pulled out a tract. She thrust it into my hands, and I finally understood what she meant.

"Where did you get this?" I asked.

"On our trip home this afternoon, we stopped for a cold drink and a restroom break. As I washed my hands I saw this on the shelf above the sink. I picked it up and glanced at it. I hope it was all right for me to take it, because in the car I read it carefully. Look! It says what you said."

I sat on the bed in shock. All I could do was marvel at the greatness of God. I marveled at His love and His provision. God and one of His obedient ones had prepared Jane's heart hours before I had the privilege of responding to her life-changing statements: "I want to be a Christian" and "Tell me what to do."

Jane had many choices. She could not choose to bring her sister back to life, but she could choose how she would respond to that day's event—the saddest day in her thirty-seven years.

Jane chose Jesus. She chose on that particular day what Jill had chosen years before. She chose life—eternal life with Christ. She could have chosen bitterness or anger or resentment. She chose just the opposite. She chose the Lord.

Have you made that choice in your life? It doesn't have to be in response to a tragedy like the death of a loved one. If, however, that is the motivation, then let it be, for the important thing is not what brings us to choose Jesus but that we choose Jesus.

Lord Jesus, I need You. Thank You for dying on the cross for my sins. I open the door of my life and receive You as my Savior and Lord. Thank You for forgiving my sins and giving me eternal life. Take control of the throne of my life. Make me the kind of person You want me to be.[14]

* * *

**One hundred years from now it won't matter if you
got that big break, took the trip to Europe,
or finally traded up to a Mercedes. . . .
It will greatly matter, one hundred years from now,
that you made a commitment to Jesus Christ.**

Author unknown

* * *

*   *   *

What good will it be for a man if he gain

the whole world, yet forfeits his soul?

Matthew 16:26

*   *   *

CHOOSE TO
Reflect

"For God so loved the world that he gave his one and only Son, that whoever believes in him shall not perish but have eternal life" (John 3:16). "The world" is you and me. It is every human being—those who love God and serve Him and those who do not. God's love for "the world" is not based on anything but His nature. We do not deserve His love and cannot earn it. He gave His love to us as He gave His only Son. When we believe in Him, in Jesus, we have eternal life.

STUDY QUESTIONS

Choose Jesus

1. Have you ever found it difficult to share the gospel with someone special? What made it challenging?
2. What person in your life needs to know Jesus? How does 1 Peter 3:15 encourage you?
3. Most often we have only a few minutes to share the gospel. Prepare a two-minute version of your testimony that outlines the gospel message. Practice by sharing it with a trusted friend. Have your friend time you!
4. Pray that the Lord would provide a divine appointment for you to share your story and the gospel message.

12

CHOOSE DAILY

Choose for yourselves this day
whom you will serve . . .
But as for me and my household,
we will serve the Lord.

JOSHUA 24:15

You often find the back half Joshua 24:15 posted on door-posts and housefronts: "As for me and my household, we will serve the Lord." It is a meaningful message, but I've always felt that the first part of the verse was potentially more significant than the last, more familiar part: "Choose for yourselves this day whom you will serve."

We are instructed to choose *this day*. Choose today whom you are going to serve. And then choose again tomorrow. One good choice does not mean you are finished; it simply means you have made one good choice. You must follow that choice with the next right choice and the next right choice after that.

*   *   *

Every experience God gives us, every person
He puts in our lives, is the perfect preparation
for the future that only He can see.
Corrie ten Boom

*   *   *

Even though the people you have read about have made godly choices, they did not make just one good choice. They have made consistent, consecutive good ones. Where are these heroines now? Let's see.

My father has been gone for more than thirty years (Choose to Forgive). I am thankful we had some degree of reconciliation before his death. I am also thankful that God has given me the choice not only to forgive but also to ask for forgiveness. Life on earth is so short. Choosing to forgive and ask for forgiveness can foster the healing of relationships and help the forgiver to live free.

Pam's daughter Emily (Choose to Pray) is cancer-free. She and her family visited Disney World, compliments of the Make-A-Wish Foundation. She also appeared in the halftime show of *Monday Night Football* to celebrate the twenty-year anniversary of the Ronald McDonald House. Emily's oldest sister managed the Ronald McDonald House in Chicago for four years before starting her own family. In 2009 Emily attended Camp-Make-a-Dream in Montana as a survivor and was asked to come back as a mentor the next summer.

Shirley's doctors told her in May of 1997 that she had only weeks to live (Choose Joy). She was instructed to plan her funeral and say goodbye to her family and friends. In October of 1997 we had lunch together. As we sat at the table marveling at what God had done, she told me she had reordered her date book subscription for 1998. In January of 1998, Shirley entered the hospice program. And on April 15, 1998, just hours before

I was to visit her, she died. Our time together was not canceled; it was merely postponed.

Betty (Choose Not to Worry) has recovered miraculously from the abuse she suffered for almost two decades. "I do not regret leaving," she told me. "I only regret that I didn't leave sooner for the sake of my children." Today Betty is married to a kind and gentle man. He is very caring and protective of her. "I am happy," Betty said. "I know that God provided for me, and He continues to do so today."

Joan (Choose to Be Content) is now the district director for a congressman in Illinois. She also serves as an elected official (trustee) in Savoy, Illinois. Elizabeth graduated from her high school special education program. She lives at home and goes to the lively home of family friends while her mom and dad are at work. Brother Phil now has a young son who loves to climb up on his aunt's wheelchair and give her kisses.

Sonnie (Choose to Respond) sold her flower shop after Eric's accident. She now owns a new business out of her home— renting wedding and party décor. Eric has a job too. For a total of six hours a week, he works at several local banks, running the paper shredder. He faithfully rides his stationary bike ten miles every day to stay in shape. He has reached a plateau in his rehabilitation.

As a result of their personal experience with J. P.'s incarceration, Carol Kent (Choose Generosity) and her husband, Gene, founded Speak Up for Hope. The vision of the not-for-profit is to help inmates and their families adjust to their new normal. Their mission is to provide hope for inmates and their families through encouragement and resources. Visit www.speakup forhope.org for more information about how you can help.

Evelina Solis (Choose to Dream) has traveled far and wide to tell her story. To follow her progress and see where the Lord is leading her, go to www.evelinasolis.com. She and her husband, Ivan, now share a dream. They want to combine their talents and education and open an authentic Mexican restaurant with healthy options for people struggling with diabetes and other health issues.

Although Lynne (Choose to Hope) is happy in her current family of three, she is very aware of the progressive nature of muscular dystrophy. Both Austin and Everett are now teenagers, and they have already lived longer than Lynne's brother who had the same disease. Someday when the boys have gone to be with the Lord, Lynne hopes for a new family, one that is ready-made and that God has prepared just for her. Whether on earth or in heaven, Lynne feels certain she will have that family.

It has been more than twenty years since Jill's death and Jane's initial commitment to Christ (Choose Jesus). Jane and I did a Bible study together by phone for more than two years. Following that time, Jane worked with her church youth group for fifteen years, putting her gifts to good use. She was recently chosen as the Big Sister of the Year in her region and serves on the advisory council for the Big Brother/Big Sister organization. Jane's daughter, Holly, is now teaching pre-kindergarten special education. Holly's strong faith reminds Jane of her sister, Jill.

*   *   *

When you look for the good in others,

you discover the best in yourself.

Martin Walsh

*   *   *

Choosing daily involves God's help, your commitment, and focus. Choosing positive, life-giving words are one way to strengthen that focus.

I taught school for several years before my husband and I started our family. One year I had a group of elementary students who did not get along well. They argued and fussed with one another almost all the time. They were respectful to me and were good listeners, but they bickered endlessly with each other.

On one especially rough day, their arguing had pushed me to the edge. I'd had it with their bad attitudes. About three minutes before recess, I asked the class to take out paper and pencils.

"Please write your name at the top of your paper," I began. "On the next line I want you to write the name of the one person you would least like to sit by. Keep your papers covered."

"Do we only write one name?" many asked.

"Can I make a list?" asked one particularly disagreeable young man.

"Just one name," I replied and paused until this part of the task was completed by everyone in class. "Now, number 1, 2, 3 on your paper and write three good things about the person you named. Write three things you could honestly praise about that person."

From the response of the students, you would have thought I had just asked them to climb Mount Everest barefoot!

"I can't!"

"That's impossible!"

Knowing something about motivation and fourth graders, I replied, "And as soon as you are done, you may go outside for recess."

Needless to say, they all completed the assignment. Now, I would like to tell you that our little exercise revolutionized the classroom, that things were never the same again, that the students had respect and appreciation for one another for the rest of the year. I would like to tell you this, but I can't because I would be lying. They did, however, treat one another more kindly for a while. It did make a positive (if not eternal) difference in their attitudes and interactions. Under my direction, those students chose to praise someone else, and the arguing subsided.

Choosing to praise another person is a good choice, one we

can make on a daily basis. Giving honest, genuine praise to others has amazing consequences. We often sport a negative attitude when we are focused on ourselves.

"I want it *my way.*"

"That's not what *I* want."

"Shouldn't that be for *me?*"

*　　*　　*

I will proclaim the name of the Lord.

Oh, praise the greatness of our God!

Deuteronomy 32:3

*　　*　　*

Focusing on someone else, praising someone else, helps to foster a positive attitude. And it is a choice. We make the choice whether or not to praise the people in our lives—and we choose this over and over again, daily. Even more importantly, we can choose to praise God. "God inhabits the praises of his people" (see Psalm 22:3). He lives there in our praises! If you ever feel removed from God, away from His presence, His Word says that if we praise Him, He is there.

The vacation Bible school kids sing a little song that talks about praising God and how much better that makes them feel. Why? Because when we praise God, we take our focus off *ourselves*, our lives, our hurts, and our desires, and shift the focus to God. That little VBS song is packed with truth.

The choices we have in life are numerous. In fact, they are so abundant that there are few things that are *not* our choice.

As a young girl I would try in vain to persuade my mother that I *had* to do something or other. To this she would consistently reply, "Kendra, there are only two things in life that you have to do. All the other things are choices. All you *have* to do is die and pay taxes!"

Maybe you heard that from your mother too. Well, today,

with respect, I would say, "Actually, all you *have* to do is die."
(Now before some IRS representative starts checking on my file,
I want to make it perfectly clear that I have chosen to pay taxes
each year of my adult life. Paying taxes is a wise choice, and it
beats high fines and jail sentences. It is, however, a choice.)

Every woman whose story appears in this book had choices
to make. So do you. Our choices are infinite in number, and
they are our daily responsibility.

We can choose joy and forgiveness. We can choose contentment and generosity. We can choose to respond, to dream,
to hope, and not to worry. We can choose prayer and Jesus. Or
we can choose to let the "if onlys" and "what ifs" of life control us.

My goal is to make the next right choice for a Christ-
centered life, just as these women did. My dream is to encourage you to do the same and to Live Free!

STUDY QUESTIONS

Choose Daily

1. Name a time when consistently making the "next right
   choice" was difficult.

2. Have you ever witnessed the positive effect of choosing to
   praise someone else?

3. God inhabits the praises of His people. Name a time you
   have witnessed His presence as you praised and worshiped
   Him.

4. Can you anticipate any time during the upcoming week
   when you might need to choose again (for example, not to
   worry, to be generous, to dream or hope)?

NOTES

TWO
Choose to Forgive

1. Jane E. Brody, "Personal Health," *New York Times*, April 12–13, 1995.

FOUR
Choose Joy

2. K. S. Peterson, "A Chuckle a Day Does Indeed Keep Ills at Bay," *USA Today* (October 31, 1996), 10D.
3. Peter Doskoch, "Happily Ever Laughter," *Psychology Today* (July 1, 1996), 32–35.
4. M. Meyer, "Laughter: It's Good Medicine," *Better Homes and Gardens* (April 1997), 72.
5. Peterson.
6. David R. Mains, "Does God Have a Sense of Humor?" *Moody Monthly* (June 1987), 60–61.

SIX
Choose to Be Content

7. Elisabeth Kubler-Ross, *On Death and Dying* (New York: Macmillan, 1969), 39.

EIGHT
Choose Generosity

8. Henry Pierson Curtis, "Blemish for Navy Officer—Murder Charge in Orlando Shooting," *Orlando Sentinel*, November 6, 1999.
9. Carol Kent, *When I Lay My Isaac Down* (Colorado Springs, CO: NavPress, 2004), 161.
10. Ibid., 26.

NINE
Choose to Dream

11. Evelina Solis, quoted in Laura Contreras-Rowe, *Aim High: Extraordinary Stories of Hispanic and Latina Women* (independently published, 2009), 50.

12. Evelina Solis, www.EvelinaSolis.com.

13. Ibid.

ELEVEN
Choose Jesus

14. Prayer from Campus Crusade for Christ, *The Four Spiritual Laws* (Peachtree, GA: Bright Media Foundation and Campus Crusade for Christ, 2007).

ACKNOWLEDGMENTS

I am very thankful to the women in each chapter of this book who have allowed me to share their stories. The joy and excitement in their voices as I told them that Moody Publishers was releasing this book reminded me of their desire to turn the negative circumstances of their lives into positive motivation for other women. Ladies, I used to say that this book was about ordinary women. Actually, godly choices are not as ordinary as we all wish they were. Thanks for following close to Jesus.

Thank you to the folks at Moody Publishers who partnered with me on this project and others through the years.

I have never written a book or prepared a message without the input of my husband, John. Your help, John, can be epitomized in Proverbs 13:14: "The teaching of the wise is a fountain of life, turning a man from the snares of death." I'm so grateful to have been your bride for more than thirty-five years.

Thanks, too, to my kids and my kids-in-law, Matthew and Marissa, Aaron and Kristin, Jonathan and Ashley—just because! You and my grandgirls make everything I do more meaningful and definitely more fun.

And of course, thank You, Jesus, for giving me something to do that is so delightful and so satisfying that it doesn't (usually) feel like work. You are truly the Author and Perfecter of my faith.

TEACHING PEOPLE HOW TO MAKE THE NEXT RIGHT CHOICE

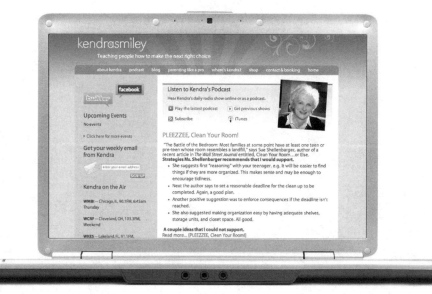

CONNECT WITH KENDRA SMILEY ONLINE

www.kendrasmiley.com